AMERICAN DREAM
THE HOUSES AT SAGAPONAC

Modern Living in the Hamptons

RIZZOLI
NEW YORK

First Published in the United States of America in 2003 by
Rizzoli International Publications, Inc.
300 Park Avenue South, New York, NY 10010

2003 2004 2005 2006 2007 / 10 9 8 7 6 5 4 3 2 1

Hardcover ISBN 0-8478-2568-X
Paperback ISBN 0-8478-2539-6
Library of Congress: 2002096036

Design by Duuplex

Printed and bound in Singapore

AMERICAN DREAM
THE HOUSES AT SAGAPONAC

Modern Living in the Hamptons

Coco Brown   Essays by Richard Meier and Alastair Gordon

CONTENTS

Introduction by Coco Brown

The idea of inviting a group of the finest architects to each build a home in one community first occurred to me twenty-five years ago in California where I had luckily and inexpensively acquired a rare 188 acre site in the low mountains that crest Beverly Hills. Here, on one of the crests, I imagined building thirty-one houses, each designed by a great modern architect, each on its own descending terrace. Early support for the idea came from my friend Richard Rogers who was then the visiting dean of architecture at UCLA; however even for this proposal of modest density the zoning process became so irrational and arduous that after some years I gave up the idea of combining art and business. At the end, we were granted 118 lots which became the successful but artless Mulholland Estates.

In the early 1990s, on the other coast's Hamptons, I was able to buy an entire "busted" subdivision, a large, attractive piece of land with all the zoning rights and improvements in place. Still harboring the idea of a community of architects, I managed to keep the lots off the market for some years. Then, one evening, I told my idea to Richard Meier, who embraced it and, after visiting the site, generously and selflessly offered to invite with me some thirty-five architects to design houses for the project. It is a measure of Richard's stature that all those invited, a mix of old masters and some of the most talented of a younger generation, accepted. The project was immediately welcomed by the architecture community and press, which enabled us to widen our perspective and invite such major stars as the great Samuel Mockbee (an inspiration whose death left us bereft) and Philip Johnson (who joined at his own request and whose house we think will survive as one of his best). We also added international participants like Shigeru Ban of Japan, Zaha Hadid of London, Winy Maas of MVRVD in the Netherlands, the Italian Antonio Citterio, France's Jean-Michel Wilmotte, and Lindy Roy, a young designer from South Africa. We now have more architects than sites, but these things, like most dinner parties, have a way of working out.

The site is located just north of the Montauk Highway in the village of Sagaponack equidistant between Southampton and East Hampton and a short drive from the ocean. The site is set apart by natural boundaries, to the south by the railroad and to the east and north by large swaths of county-owned nature reserves. Wide country lanes already exist, and the woods they run through are home to tall, mature trees, so that each house would be framed discreetly from its neighbor. The site includes a thirteen-acre reserve, which will belong to the homeowners' association, with walking paths, individual vegetable gardens, a tree farm, and a center for the community of homeowners. This development

is an anti-subdivision, the opposite of the usual, shoddy conformist repetition that has made the very word subdivision a pejorative. Our intent with the Houses at Sagaponac is to allow a diverse community to evolve, where the houses express the individual voices of each architect and homeowner.

After the acceptances we sent out an "owner's brief" to each architect in which we requested "restraint of gesture" (avoiding the tendencies of one kind of modernism which overlooks basic elements like closets and physical spaces where human bodies must interact and reside), "modesty of size" (a criterion intended as an antidote to the oversize houses then flooding the market), a sense of introspection, respect for the country setting, and an unpretentious, even fun, sensibility.

Over the last thirty months we have been reviewing, editing, and engineering all the designs, together with the architects. As might be expected, the designs are all at different stages. Some designs will not be built. Others are only in draft form, while still others have been carried all the way through final construction documents to building department approval, and will start construction this spring. The project keeps evolving, a work in progress, visible on the website, *www.housesatsagaponac.com*.

Still the task has been more daunting than I had imagined. Even with the help of our team: our builder Ronan O'Dwyer, our engineers Robert Silman Associates, and especially our team of in-house architects, Paula Willson, Sunitha Ramachandran, Jayda Uras and Peggy Hsu, I have often felt overcommitted. I have had occasion to ask myself: Why do this? Why (and how) can I field and edit the projects of thirty-five stars in a field in which I have never even taken a class? I have been devoted to the arts—but other arts: theater, film and literature. Still, I felt unqualified for the job, an interloper, assigned for reasons I did not understand to the role of benign catalyst; a Prufrock, deferential, glad to be of use. I think the results of the interaction have been positive, creative, and rewarding—most work improves under the influence of a client or an editor. My friend Jacquelin Robertson says, "Good architecture is made by good clients. Without them, it is like pushing against cotton." My training in literary criticism has also proven useful—I try to identify the basic idea, drive, or metaphor of each house, and encourage its development; and at the same time to make the house buildable, affordable, and practical ("Where is the laundry room?").

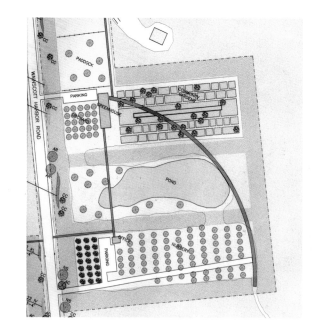

Houses at Sagaponac

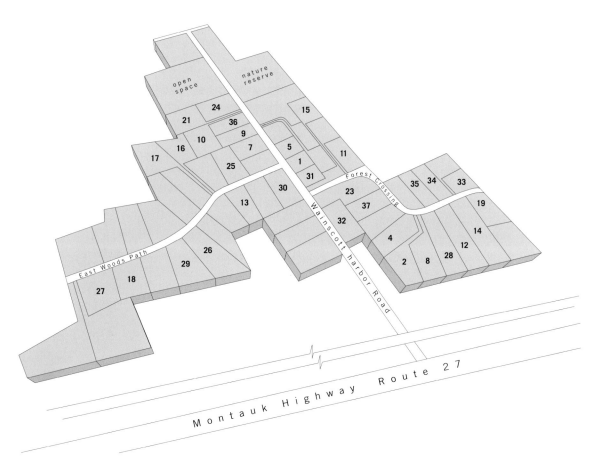

1 Stan Allen
2 Marwan Al-Sayed
3 Anthony Ames
4 Shigeru Ban & Dean Maltz
5 Deborah Berke
6 Antonio Citterio with Patricia Viel
7 Henry N. Cobb
8 Francois de Menil
9 James Ingo Freed
10 Richard Gluckman
11 Michael Graves
12 Zaha Hadid
13 Thomas Hanrahan & Victoria Meyers
14 Gisue Hariri & Mojgan Hariri
15 Steven Harris
16 Craig Hodgetts & Hsin-ming Fung
17 Steven Holl
18 Carlos Jimenez
19 Philip Johnson & Alan Ritchie
20 Robert Kahn
21 Stephen H. Kanner
22 John Keenen & Terence Riley
23 Richard Meier
24 Samuel Mockbee
25 Eric Owen Moss
26 Winy Maas, Jacob van Rijs & Nathalie de Vries
27 Thomas Phifer
28 Jesse Reiser & Nanako Umemoto
29 Jaquelin Robertson
30 Richard Rogers
31 Michael Rotondi & Clark Philipp Stevens
32 Daniel Rowen
33 Lindy Roy
34 Annabelle Selldorf
35 Henry Smith-Miller & Laurie Hawkinson
36 Calvin Tsao & Zach McKown
37 Jean-Michel Wilmotte

I imagine living in the different houses, as a conservative thinker, a "swinging" bachelor, a father of four, or an empty nester, envisioning an environment particular to each role I assume, which brings me to the answer of why I have undertaken this. It is a form of personal existential greed that pulled me into real estate in the first place. I never visit anyplace without looking at houses or land to buy, even if I do not want to live there, because in the process I get to imagine living in all these places, and thus I can—like an actor—multiply my one, little existence into many different lives. There is another illusory motive and that is the ambition, long harbored, to create and leave something of lasting importance, even if it isn't one's own creation. Finally, this project gratifies my old love of rebellion. You cannot imagine a place of more self-conscious conformity than Southampton, where men still dress for dinner in blue blazers and velvet slippers, and where the houses (even as they are primarily drawn from the culturally diverse population of contemporary New York) are mostly ersatz imitations of eighteenth- and nineteenth-century mansions, times whose mores and building styles are defunct. These houses, once hidden behind high hedges in hypocritical decorum, like bejeweled dowagers, are now displaying themselves in the same style, but built larger than ever on postage-stamp-size lots. Our community of well-designed, modestly sized modern houses may be upsetting to the status quo, just as we see some members of the local architecture-review board spoiling to reject these designs, despite the designers' preeminent qualifications and despite the discreet, wooded location of the project.

Now with the design process well under way, we have begun construction. Already the Hariri and Hariri house is rising, framed on its great plinth like a stage elevated among the tall pines. Neighboring it on one side will be Zaha Hadid's house, and Philip Johnson's on the other side. I imagine walking down this wide country lane, passing the Hadid, Al-Sayed, and Johnson houses on one side, and the Roy, Selldorf, Smith-Miller/Hawkinson, and Graves houses on the other, and I think, no one will have seen anything quite like this.

Will they be as beautiful and strong as we imagine? Will people buy them? Will the homeowners be happy there? Will the result be as much a new paradigm as we hope? Ultimately, the proof of this dream—call it Utopian Idealism—will be in the pudding, or in the "building," and "dwelling" to use Heidegger's words. "Will these houses actually get built?" ask skeptics. The answer to that question is a resounding yes.

Domestic Architecture Reborn by Aric Chen

The Houses at Sagaponac are uniquely—even disarmingly—optimistic. It is not simply that, in a real estate market that favors bloated historicism, these homes on the affluent east end of Long Island will have to be sold as modestly sized and rather aggressively modern structures. Nor is it because, alongside well-established architects, some relatively untried talents will be tested with their first major commissions. Instead, what may be most extraordinary about the Houses at Sagaponac is that they attempt to foretell a broader future for domestic architecture.

Recent decades have eroded much faith in architecture in general, particularly in the United States. Deflated by the failed, mid-twentieth-century experiments of modernism—urban renewal, monolithic public housing projects, empty windswept plazas—the profession found its social mandate largely discredited by the late 1970s. It retreated inward and occupied itself with self-referential explorations best exemplified by the decorative reappropriations of 1980s postmodernism. Though that also fell out of favor, even recent blockbuster projects—Frank Gehry's Guggenheim Bilbao, for example, or Rem Koolhaas' New York flagship for Prada—can, by themselves, claim a social efficacy that might be reduced to that of public spectacle.

Where, then, do the Houses at Sagaponac fit in? Certainly, and intentionally, the concentration of talent is spectacular. But they have also been equated, however superficially, with precedents that loom large in the history of modern housing. Among these are Germany's Weissenhofsiedlung of the 1920s and the California Case Study Houses of the postwar era. In the former Stuttgart development, Mies van der Rohe, Le Corbusier, Walter Gropius, and others created mixed-income residences to advocate modernism's social potential during a time of housing shortages. In the latter, on sites scattered throughout the Los Angeles area, the likes of Richard Neutra, Charles and Ray Eames, and Eero Saarinen constructed daring examples of affordable modern homes for a country immersed in a building boom.

Both programs mirror the Houses at Sagaponac as impressive assemblages of well-known architects. But the Houses at Sagaponac, designed for the upper and upper-middle classes, differ fundamentally from the prior populist efforts. In addition, the earlier projects were steeped in utopianism, encouraged by the architects' belief that something approaching a panacea had been found within the strictures of modernism. No such claims are being made in

Sagaponac, nor could they be. Instead, this undertaking represents a more discrete kind of utopia, primarily defined by its opposition to the status quo, and bolstered by the faith that something new—whatever form it might take—is still possible.

Accordingly, the Houses at Sagaponac are distinguished by their aesthetic pluralism. To be sure, their architects have been chosen by only developer Harry Brown and architect Richard Meier. However, appropriately for our time, there is no clear ideological bond that joins them. For instance, the house by Craig Hodgetts and Hsin Ming Fung is a deconstructivist glass cube, with a retractable wall, that's punctured by curving walls and off-angle boxes. Eric Owen Moss, who once worked with Frank Gehry, designed a twisting, contorted volume that irrevocably distorts and mutates the modern box. The houses by Lindy Roy and Zaha Hadid both express the language of digital design in dynamic, fluid structures, though with very different results.

Others are rooted in a more classic modernist idiom. Shigeru Ban devised a restrained structure that elegantly extends outward along a Cartesian grid. John Keenen and Terence Riley have bifurcated the single home, creating two simple, rectangular structures in its stead, while formalizing the outdoor space that results in-between them.

The Houses at Sagaponac are thus representative of the diversity that characterizes contemporary architectural practice. They range from the starkly rectilinear to the vigorously organic. They find their influences in everything from quintessential modernism and minimalism to deconstructivism, from the vernacular to the digitally-inspired. There is even room for postmodernism—Michael Graves's classically-organized villa and the Pantheon-inspired domes of Philip Johnson and Alan Ritchie.

Also worth mentioning is the diversity of the architects themselves. They come from both coasts of the United States, and throughout Europe and Japan. Many are veteran practitioners, while others will be seeing their first major projects constructed. Even the experienced will mark milestones. For example, both Henry Cobb and James Ingo Freed—who have been partners with I.M. Pei for nearly fifty years—are building their first houses ever. Interestingly, the two colleagues' contributions are strikingly dissimilar: Cobb's is a soberingly cloistered house, inspired by the work of minimalist sculptor Donald Judd, while Freed's is a more lively and compact composition of boxes, vaults and curves.

Indeed, if the Houses at Sagaponac are didactic, that didacticism resides in the diversity of their designs. Idiosyncratic as individual creations, collectively they react to a mundane context by substantiating its multifarious alternative; their social relevance lies in the breadth of their proximate numbers. Architecture is hunkering down here, literally regrouping to exercise an influence that is not predetermined but indeterminately inevitable. And importantly, it's doing so in the domestic realm.

Perhaps the late, and extraordinarily inventive, Samuel Mockbee understood all of this when he accepted Brown's invitation to design a house. Presented with the project, Mockbee—a somewhat unlikely participant, having earned his considerable reputation designing for Alabama's rural poor—first asked "Will it be a gated community?" Informed that it wouldn't, and realizing its experimental potential, Mockbee agreed to participate. Encouraging better housing models for the rich cannot be separated from doing the same for the poor, Mockbee seemed to say. Architecture's influence may not always transcend socioeconomic boundaries, but it can extend across them, if only subtly.

Years after his involvement at Weissenhofsiedlung, Walter Gropius maintained that "A modern, harmonic and lively architecture is the visible sign of authentic democracy." The Houses at Sagaponac are, in their different ways, doubtlessly modern; they are surely lively; and in their heterogeneity, they are harmonic in a way that contradicts Gropius's intended meaning, but in so doing are, however imperfectly, truer to his words.

Returning to Long Island by Richard Meier

The Houses at Sagaponac present a unique opportunity to show one way in which a typical American residential subdivision can support high-quality architecture related to our time and to its particular place.

Coco Brown explained to me that he owned thirty-five more or less contiguous building sites—something rare in the Hamptons—in a wooded, secluded, and relatively undistinguished area. He suggested this might be a rare opportunity to build a community of modern homes and asked me to help him determine a way of building to achieve excellence in design with the best of a younger generation of architects.

It seemed to me that this was an opportunity for young architects to show what they were capable of doing. We chose them based on the quality of their unbuilt projects as much as for the distinction of their built work. It seemed logical that the architects be based on the East Coast, relatively near to Long Island. But in order to widen the reach of the project beyond its locale, architects were chosen from California, Arizona, England, and elsewhere. Subsequently, not all of the architects who were invited to participate chose to do so, leaving some sites available for a few who are not so young, and one who is a great old-timer.

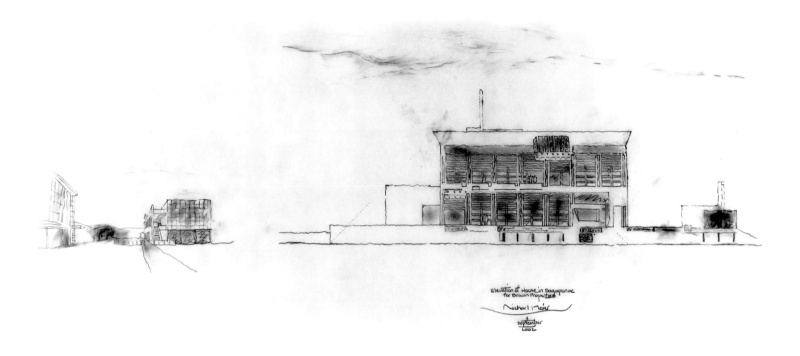

Elevation of House in Sagaponac
for Brown Properties

Michael Meier

3
September
2002

The houses are located in Sagaponack, a small village in the Town of Southampton, a community on the east end of Long Island where many New Yorkers spend relaxing weekends and holidays close to the ocean. The sites are each about one and a half to two acres in size. Historically this part of the Hamptons has been blighted by inordinately large and generally derivative "spec" houses. In contrast, the intention for the Houses at Sagaponac is to design innovative houses with reasonable square footage and sales price.

What happened, and what I expected would happen, was that a certain comraderie as well as competitiveness among the architects ensued. Each architect had the opportunity to design a dream house of sorts—to explore his or her own ideas and think about future inhabitants who would eventually move in. Although almost all of the architects selected might be loosely categorized as "modern," the sense of modernity that pervades the house designs does not come from a prescribed manifesto. The results are intended to be provocative, but not necessarily quirky, flamboyant or irrational.

People have expressed their interest in living in one of the Sagaponac Houses because they think the concept is intriguing, the mix of architects is dynamic, and it is bound to become an interesting and diverse community—a place where they could imagine living.

Certainly, there is the desire on the part of all involved to create a unique place, and in that sense, a paradigm of civilization and hopefully, a community that demonstrates different standards from those encountered in typical subdivisions. It is possible to think this kind of innovation might reach shores other than those of Long Island.

The whole endeavor is like planting multiple seeds in a garden. The sun will shine, you pray for rain and hopefully the harvest will be fruitful and abundant. Time will tell.

Modernism on Long Island by Alastair Gordon

It would be easy to draw parallels between the Houses at Sagaponac and the Case Study houses of Southern California, but it's not necessary to go so far afield. This group of houses—this American seidlung—is the continuation of a dialogue that started on eastern Long Island as far back as the 1920s when experimental ideas first washed ashore from Europe. Something in the sea-reflected light and sandy landscape called out for architecture with a capital A. There were the startling beach cabanas in Hamptons Bays (1930) by William Muschenheim who had studied with Peter Behrens in Vienna; even an incongruous prairie style house atop the Montauk bluffs, the Carera Beach House (1940), by Antonin Raymond, a former associate of Frank Lloyd Wright.

During World War II, gasoline was rationed and the area was overlooked. But near the end of the war, a young Robert Motherwell followed the migration of Surrealist poets and artists who were discovering the region, and moved to East Hampton. In 1946, Motherwell built a Quonset house with Pierre Chareau and painted the first of his Spanish Elegies there. Jackson Pollock, who had turned a barn into a studio, made some of his first drip paintings on its floor. Le Corbusier came in 1950 to visit the Italian sculptor Costantino Nivola. He painted a mural in Nivola's house and made plaster castings on the beach.

The Hamptons became a testing ground for new ideas. Boundaries seemed to dissolve in the relaxed atmosphere of beach parties and summer light. Frederick Kiesler, just a mile up the road from Pollock, worked on his "Endless House" project, a free-flowing space in which all ends would meet, "and meet continuously." Kiesler condemned the traditional house as being a "voluntary prison." Tony Smith, the architect/artist took a first step towards pure sculpture with the house and studio he designed for Theodoros Stamos: a free-standing, hexagonal extrusion raised on pylons and aimed towards the sea.

BELOW Robert Motherwell in a Quonset house designed by Pierre Chareau, East Hampton, NY, 1948 (photo: Hans Namuth)

RIGHT Carera Beach House designed by Antonin Raymond, Montauk, NY, 1940

OPPOSITE Le Corbusier painting a mural at the Nivola house, Amagansett, NY, 1950 (courtesy Ruth Nivola)

Meanwhile, a new breed of Hamptonites was arriving on the scene. They were young professionals, what one writer called "prosperous bohemians." They liked to rub shoulders with the artists but had weekday jobs in the city—in publishing, psychoanalysis, advertising, radio, and television. They were coming for solitude, for inner peace, and a dry martini, but eastern Long Island was never Walden. It was a place to see and be seen, to measure oneself against other New Yorkers.

The prosperous bohemians expressed themselves by building modernist houses—what one magazine called "flat-roofed blisters," upsetting figure-ground conventions just as Pollock had done with paint. Architects of choice included George Nelson, Robert Rosenberg, Philip Johnson, Gordon Bunshaft, Andrew Geller, and Julian and Barbara Neski—who all saw the beachfront setting as a blank sheet of paper on which to experiment. They were delighted to find clients willing to take risks: "When it is a vacation house, even conservative homeowners are likely to accept an unusual form," reported *Life* in 1959.

The beach houses of this period were not only ways to escape the city, but equally important, ways to escape the past. They were simple, seasonal, inexpensive to build and maintain, not the mega-investments of recent years. They had small kitchens, sliding glass doors, and broad sun decks spilling out over the sand. Philip Johnson's Farney House (1946) was a simple wood-and-glass pavilion in the Breuer mold, perched on the dunes of Sagaponack. It should not be lost to posterity that Johnson designed this, one of his first projects, and is now designing one of the Houses at Sagaponac.

RIGHT outdoor living room at the Holiday House,
Quogue, NY, George Nelson architect, 1950
(photo by Ezra Stoller © ESTO)

OPPOSITE Holiday House at night (photo by
George Nelson/Jacqueline Nelson Collection)

RIGHT cover of *American Home,* July 1954,
showing the Lewis beach house in Springs, NY,
Robert Rosenberg architect

BELOW the Pin Wheel House, 1954, Water Mill, NY,
Peter Blake architect (photo courtesy of Peter Blake)

OPPOSITE (top) Farney House, 1946, Sagaponack, NY,
Philip Johnson architect (photo by Ezra Stoller © ESTO)

OPPOSITE (bottom) Sagaponac House 19,
Philip Johnson & Alan Ritchie architects

In 1954, Peter Blake designed a weekend retreat in Water Mill with walls that could slide open on all sides to resemble a pin wheel. The small, twenty-four by twenty-four foot house was nothing but view. When his family expanded, Blake built two twenty-four by twenty-four foot boxes in Bridgehampton and attached them with a breezeway aimed like the lens of a camera at the bay. In some cases, the originality of design grew from a view denied, as with the Johnson House (East Hampton, 1952) where George Nelson devised a house with crisscrossing ramps to reach above a public bathing pavilion and "steal" the ocean view.

By the 1960s, the final section of the Long Island Expressway (LIE) was nearing completion, delivering more people as well as a more frenetic kind of energy. Allan Kaprow and other New York artists organized "happenings" on the beaches and the Hamptons were marketed as a multi-media event. Houses by a younger generation of architects like Richard Meier and Charles Gwathmey were gestural and vertical, more urban in temperament than the flat-roofed blisters of Blake and Bunshaft. In the 1960s rage for personal fulfillment, they were seen as transformational (almost spiritual) devices with their thin planar surfaces and transparent volumes—like architectural encounter groups.

In the 1980s, basic values seemed to change. Artists, and writers who had come in the 1950s sold their waterfront lots to stockbrokers, and with the change, the innocence of the early beach days was lost. Historicism, often pastiche, became the official Hamptons style, expressing "arrival," social status, and abundance. The relationship between

ABOVE Sabel House, Bridgehampton, NY,
Julian and Barbara Neski, architects, 1970
(Courtesy: Julian and Barbara Neski)

OPPOSITE Sagaponac House 14,
Gisue Hariri & Mojgan Hariri

inside and outside became suburbanized: flaring sun decks turned into Victorian porches, walls of sheer glass were papered over with Chinoiserie, views were squeezed through Palladian windows and the natural landscape was micro-managed with computerized irrigation systems. But by the end of the old millenium one could already detect a yearning for new directions and this brings us to the Houses at Sagaponac.

The very notion of leisure has changed profoundly in recent years. To be sure, the thirty-odd proposals for Sagaponac go beyond the bunk-bed simplicity of the post-war period. These houses are intensely urban artifacts and reconfigure the meaning of "weekend." The velvet handcuffs of the digital age follow us to the most distant extremities. The buffer between work and "downtime" is virtually nonexistent while the circuit between city and country becomes a mobius strip of perpetual expectation.

Since Thorstein Veblen published his Theory of the Leisure Class in 1899, the vacation house has been seen to signify the aspirations and uncertainties of American power. The shingled trophies of the 80s/90s boom appropriated content from 19th century robber barons. In the post-9/11 era such conspicuous displays of wealth seem misplaced, even offensive. While utopian idealism has been expelled from the discourse, there is a luminous lightness to the houses at Sagaponac that is both encouraging and cathartic. Beyond mere salesmanship, their programs suggest a Hamptons lifestyle that is less dependent on status.

Many appear to hover above the earth on veils of translucent matter. Some convey a voyeuristic tendency that is less gender specific than the bachelor-pad eroticism of Geller and Nelson. Certainly, there is penetration and collision of formal elements. There is also a thinness of surface that echoes the tautly wrapped geometries of the 1960s.

Gwathmey's house for his parents (Amagansett, 1965) and Meier's Saltzman house (East Hampton, 1969) foretold a decade of rupture. The houses at Sagaponac, as yet unbuilt, foretell a decade of change that is still too young to anticipate. While some arrive by helicopter, most still get to the Hamptons by automobile, a dystopian experience that can resonate through an entire weekend. The frame of view is, in a sense, predetermined by the windshield of one's car heading east from the city. The carport becomes the formal point of entry and the house is reduced to a narrow interface between highway and nature. In the house by Smith-Miller + Hawkinson, the car slips under a cantilevered deck "internalizing and showcasing the automobile." Mobility is further developed as a theme in the house by Zaha Hadid which becomes its own high-speed landscape, while the house by Jesse Reiser and Nanako Umemoto resembles the curving segment of a highway off-ramp. Arrival and departure merge into a single refrain, as if these houses were offering the briefest moment of suspension before directing the homeowner back towards Manhattan.

All are objects placed in the natural setting, built on lots of varying sizes. Some architects engaged the flat woodlands to their advantage while others created artificial landscapes. Calvin Tsao and Zack McKown carved out a sunken pool beneath which the glass cube of their house appears to rotate. A "secret gallery" runs beneath a T-shaped pool in Steven Holl's proposal. A lap pool penetrates the facade of Lindy Roy's house and merges with an indoor waterfall.

There is a borrowing of natural elements as in Annabelle Selldorf's "micro landscape" or the hedgelike form of Thomas Phifer's house. Others direct their gestures upwards towards sunlight and the sea-flecked sky: a landscaped roof on Steven Harris's house; a sod roof on Steven Holl's house. A prismatic roof draws daylight into the house by

Marwan Al-Sayed while "monitor" type skylights do the same for Stan Allen's house. Some structures are raised above ground level, propped on plinths like Steven Kanner's house or given elevated decks and roof terraces as in Henry Cobb's. The house by the Dutch firm MVRDV hovers above the treetops like a rain forest spa, straining for a view of the distant sea itself. Seen as a group, a kind of "anti-Seaside," the houses at Sagaponac engage in a loosely ordered dialogue between city and country, inside and outside, work and leisure. Downtime may take the form of quiet meditation or extreme physical exertion, like parasurfing, or the hyper kind of networking that prevails in the Hamptons. Some seem to look inward and outward at the same time. They are open, yet protected by different kinds of devices for screening or filtering as in the lath chrysalis surrounding the house by RoTo Architects, or the retractable wall of glass in the Hodgetts/Fung house. Metal shutters slide across the glass facade of Hariri & Hariri's L-shaped house to reveal or conceal "hidden motivations."

The return of the gable and picket fence started as an academic pun in the late 1960s, but it became a moral crusade in the Hamptons of the 1980s when realtors began warning their clients to hire only "traditionalists" if they wanted easy resale. There was constant talk about a "sense of place" and "hearth" and similar sentiments. The Houses at Sagaponac are as much about speed and turn-around time as they are about hearth. A sense of place has given way to a sense of perpetual motion that mirrors the odd condition of our times. The idea of modernity may still seem monolithic, but acknowledging it allows us to peer, however warily, into the future without flinching.

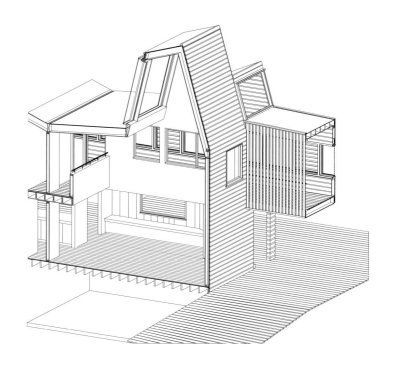

STAN ALLEN

Field Operations   Sagaponac House 1   3,200 sq ft

Sagaponac House 1 was conceived by Stan Allen as a light and informal weekend house, open to and integrated with the landscape. To this end, Allen designed a courtyard house with a simple, compact footprint. The active roofline and wood cladding recall local vernacular traditions, while the open floor plan and interlocking of solid and void acknowledge contemporary lifestyles. The patchwork site plan creates a series of intermediate spaces for outdoor living. Outdoor courts and gardens are integrated into the living spaces, folding the site into the house. Generous glass walls open to the deck, which connects directly to the pool. Filtered, ambient light that changes with the seasons and the time of day fills the house from the roof lights and from the louvers, screens, and battens located at the house's perimeter.

ABOVE axonometric section
OPPOSITE approach view

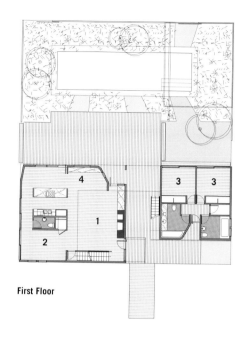

First Floor

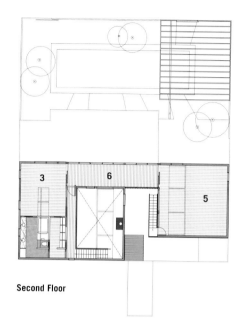

Second Floor

1 living room
2 dining room
3 bedroom
4 library
5 studio
6 screened porch

OPPOSITE interior perspective of living room
ABOVE floor plans
RIGHT model, aerial view

LEFT aerial view of entry
BELOW elevations
OPPOSITE garden perspective

MARWAN AL-SAYED

Marwan Al-Sayed Architects, Ltd. Sagaponac House 2 3,700 sq ft

Most interested in a building's relationship to the sun and sky, Marwan Al-Sayed was struck by the density of the forested site and the absence of direct light from the forest floor. Al-Sayed addressed this by clearing a south-facing oval form on the site to create a natural courtyard that welcomes sun and sky: by focusing on the immense power of the sun, he connects the house to nature and the elements. The house stands in contrast to the dense forest surrounding it, especially at night, when the house glows from within. The demands of luxury, leisure, and play prompted the architect to bathe the house in various qualities of light, both natural and artificial, to create an emotional space for relaxing, entertaining, and living.

The building is oriented to the south to maximize the available sunlight created by the oval clearing. The plan is characterized by a series of long, continuous skylights that filter light down into the house's series of elongated, vaulted surfaces creating different qualities and colors of light, thereby accentuating various functions in the house—eating, bathing, or sleeping. Although the house's overall form is simple, Al-Sayed creates a mysterious, sensual play of light that imparts a feeling of retreat and luxury.

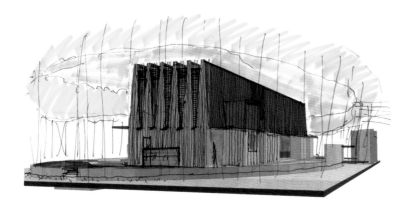

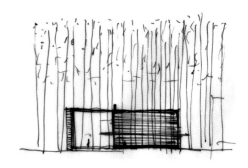

ABOVE (left & right) sketches
OPPOSITE interior perspective, living room

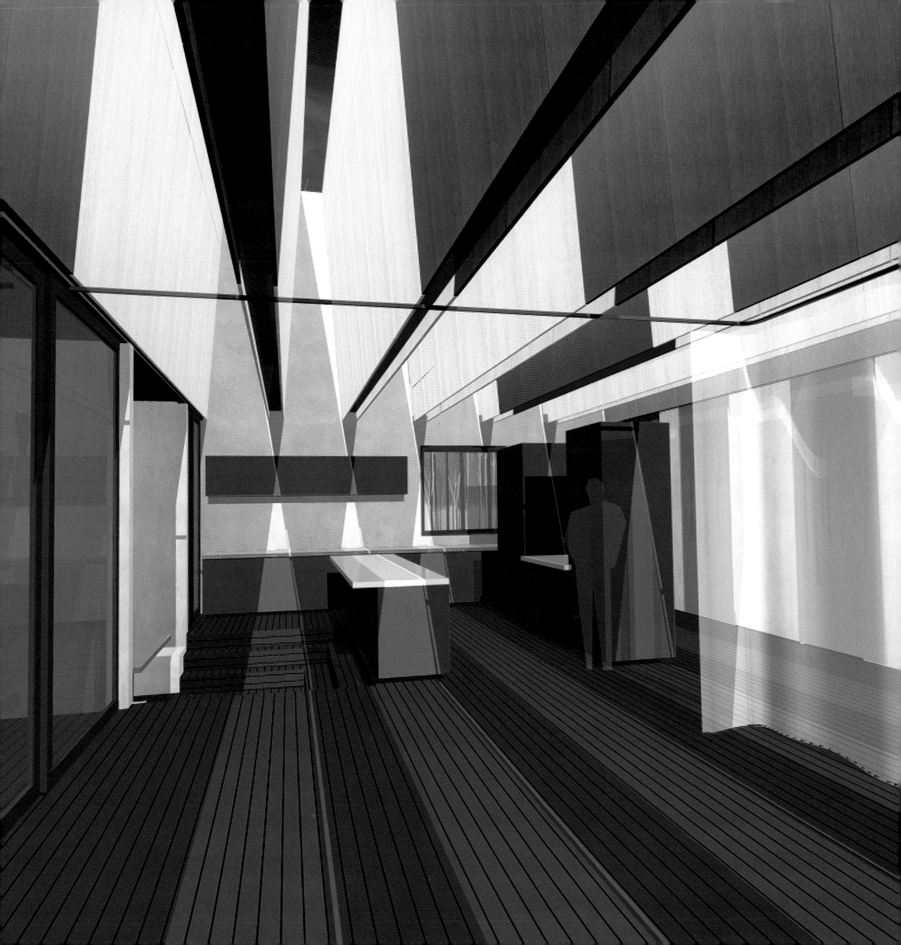

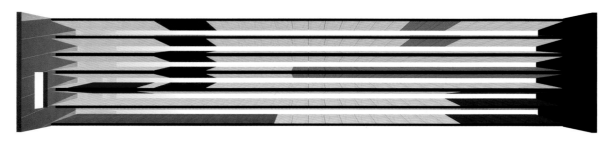

ABOVE light study, interior view and ceiling
OPPOSITE light study, interior view

33

RIGHT light study, interior views at night
BELOW light study, section showing colored lights

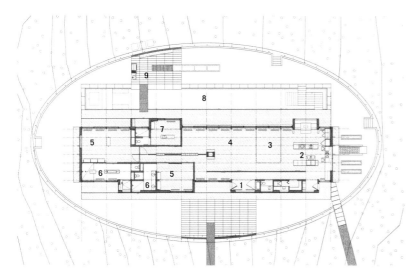

1 entrance
2 kitchen
3 dining room
4 living room
5 bedroom
6 bathroom
7 guest room/cabana
8 pool
9 patio

RIGHT sketch, house in forest
BELOW model, birdseye view
OPPOSITE exterior perspecitve, daytime

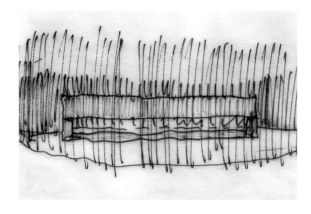

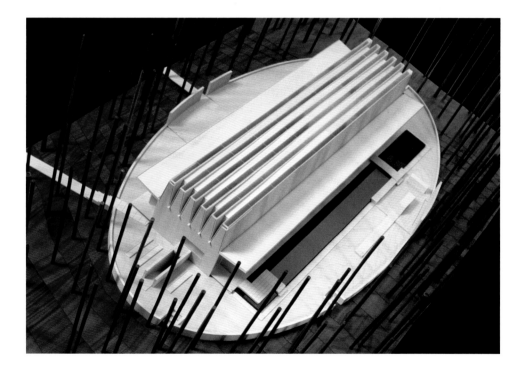

ANTHONY AMES

Anthony Ames Architect   Sagaponac House 3   3,000 - 3,600 sq ft

Sagaponac House 3 is part of a larger site strategy that emphasizes the separation of the house from the landscape by raising it slightly and placing it on the corner of a large plinth. This flat area would have ground cover, be paved, or provide a place for a swimming pool or other outdoor activities. A garage adjacent to the parking court acts as an element of definition for this area. Sagaponac House 3 is a single-story square with the major spaces arranged around a small glazed court. Approximately one half of the perimeter wall is floor-to-ceiling glass; the other half is white stucco. Upon entry one encounters a view through the glazed court, through the living/dining area, across the terrace and pool, to the landscape beyond. Attached to the main square of the house by a corridor is a second bedroom, which forms a courtyard space shared with the main house. The bedrooms each have distinct characteristics. One is remote and secluded, the other is open and engages the landscape. Two additional bedrooms located above the main volume, are also an option.

Containment and enclosure alternate with expansion and release as one enters the site and the house. The house and garage form a closed condition at the end of a long drive, and the entry further compresses space. Release to an open vista through the house occurs as one moves into the house. A condition of repose is achieved in the contained area between the house and the master bedroom. From here one can enjoy the contrast of the pure geometry of the formalized planted and paved plinth with the natural condition of forest, just beyond.

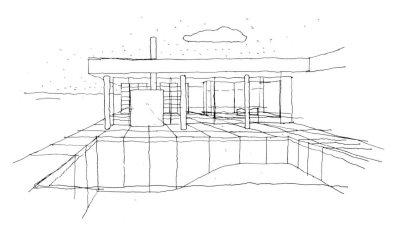

LEFT sketch showing pool
OPPOSITE view from entry

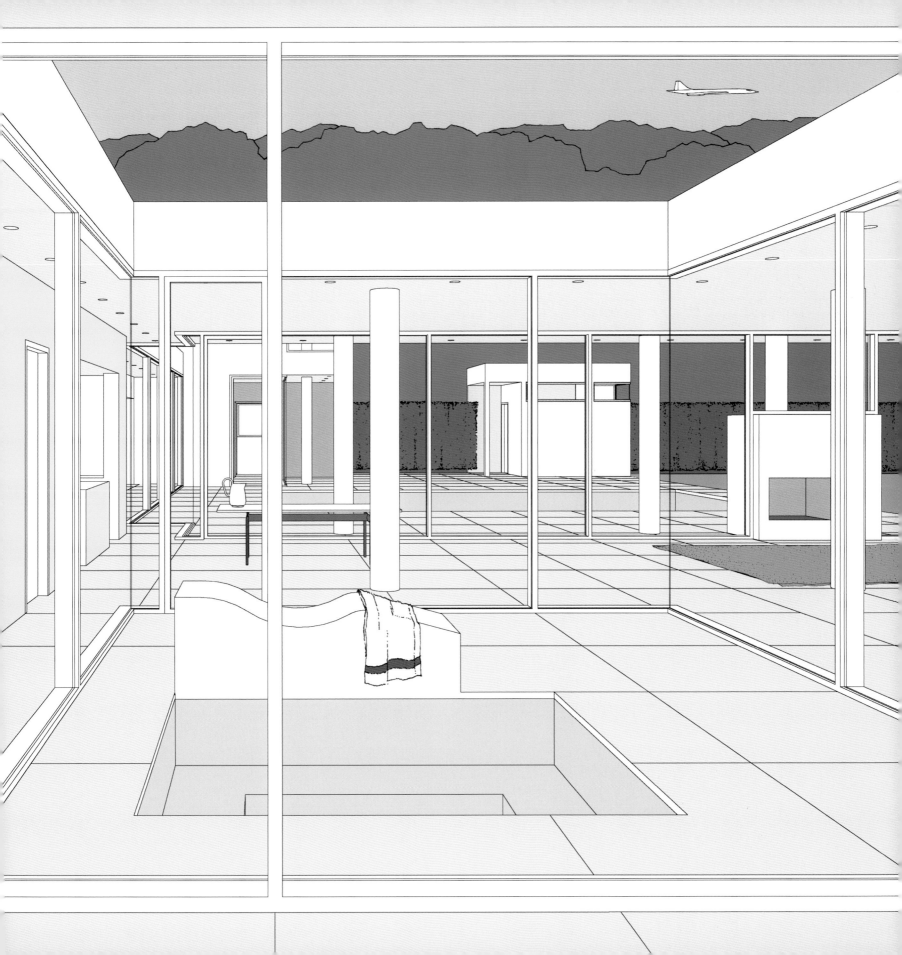

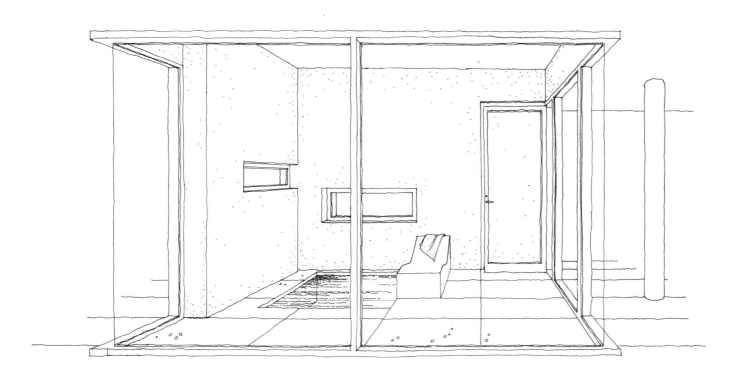

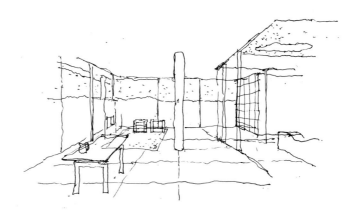

ABOVE (top) view of atrium looking north
ABOVE (bottom) sketch of living room from kitchen

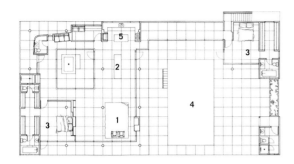

First Floor

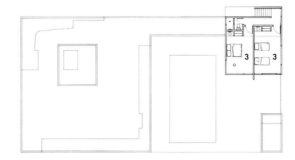

Second Floor

1 living room
2 dining room
3 bedroom
4 pool
5 kitchen

ABOVE floor plans
RIGHT exploded axonometric
OVERLEAF elevational perspective

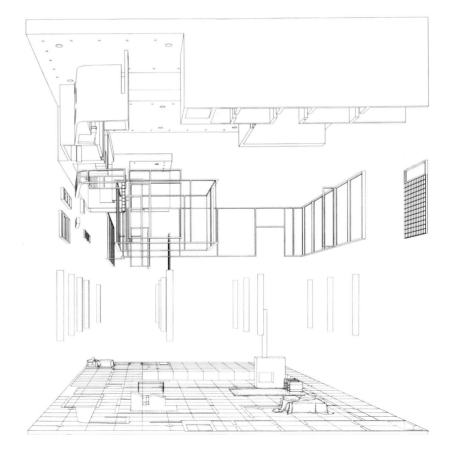

SHIGERU BAN & DEAN MALTZ

Shigeru Ban Architects + Dean Maltz Architect   Sagaponac House 4   3,800 sq ft

Shigeru Ban's design for Sagaponac House 4 employs a spatial division of the house into four separate zones of public and private use. This geometric approach is derived from an analysis of the open space planning used by Mies van der Rohe in his unbuilt Brick Country House. The plan of Sagaponac House 4 is first divided into two halves by a north-south wall separating the public and private realms. The two halves are further divided into quadrants by an intersecting east-west wall. Each of these four zones is enriched by an individual garden that integrates the interior with the surrounding landscape. The contrasting relationships between interior space and exterior garden create four unique qualities of space and landscape.

The house is also informed by an innovative approach to mass production, in part inspired by the early modernists' experiments with standardization and cost control. The structural system of the house is founded on the early-twentieth-century explorations of standardization and mass production as efficient means of achieving a highly engineered product. The mass-produced structure for Sagaponac House 4 is composed of a system of furniture units.

The furniture in this house is not traditionally imagined, designed, or executed. It is comprised of modular, full-height furniture units that become elements of structural support, spatial division and storage (closets, bookcases, cabinetry, lighting, and packaged HVAC units). Because the furniture units are prefabricated in a controlled factory environment, no skilled workers are needed on site for furniture production. These units work as a modular system in which two people can move, position, and install each piece. The furniture is prefinished on the interior and exterior. If a furniture unit composes an exterior wall, sheathing is applied for waterproofing and insulation. Shigeru Ban's development of structural furniture began in 1983 and to date four Furniture Houses have been built in Japan and China. The remaining building systems include site-built floor slabs, roof, and curtain wall glazing. In total, the planning combines open interior and exterior spaces and inventive, simple building components proportioned to the human scale.

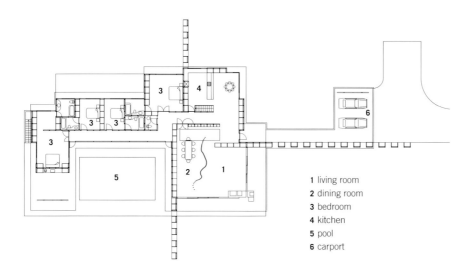

1 living room
2 dining room
3 bedroom
4 kitchen
5 pool
6 carport

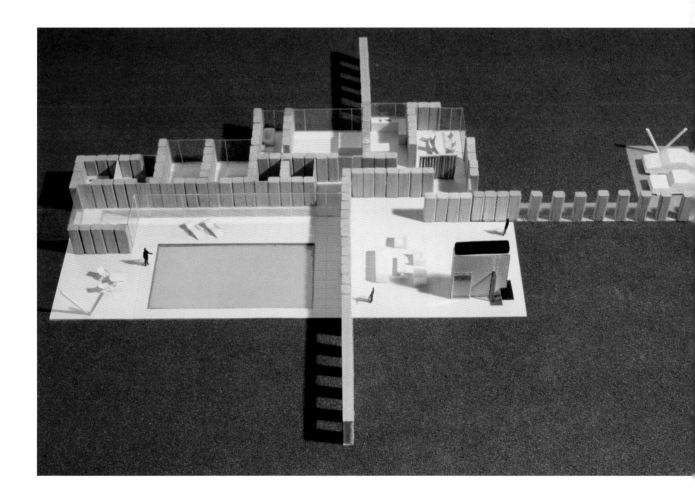

ABOVE furniture unit

RIGHT aerial view of model
without roof

OPPOSITE aerial view of model

DEBORAH BERKE

Deborah Berke & Partners Architects, LLP   Sagaponac House 5   3,100 sq ft

The site of Sagaponac House 5, shielded from its neighbors amidst undisturbed woodlands on the edge of the development, inspired Deborah Berke Architects to leave the majority of the land untouched and to design a simple, understated summer refuge reminiscent of reductivist beach houses of the 1960s and 1970s. Clean, simple materials—Alaskan yellow cedar siding and stucco on the chimney—complement the landscape and will weather with nuance and texture. Above the main entrance, the top of a trellis peeks over the flat roofs and pure volumes, providing a subtle clue to the refuge within.

The main entrance leads visitors into the house and its central court, at which point the house reveals its character as an oasis in the woods. The U-shaped plan and abundant windows direct inhabitants inward toward the court, which in turn beckons them outdoors to a swimming pool and space for relaxing and entertaining. Stairs ascend from the court to a roof deck situated above the entrance, providing a more intimate outdoor space. The interior details—Royal Danbury marble in the bathrooms, a zinc-paneled fireplace, and painted wood floors—echo regional traditions and reinforce the design approach: to realize a humane modernism appropriate to a summer escape.

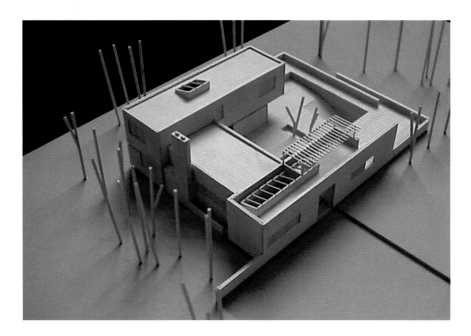

ABOVE front elevation
OPPOSITE aerial view of model

ABOVE courtyard perspective
OPPOSITE floor plans

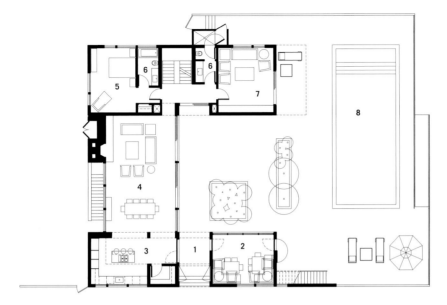

1 entry porch
2 screened porch
3 kitchen
4 livingroom/dining
5 bedroom
6 bathroom
7 studio/guest
8 pool
9 roof terrace

First Floor

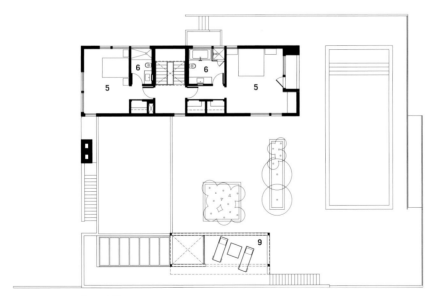

Second Floor

51

ANTONIO CITTERIO WITH PATRICIA VIEL

Antonio Citterio and Partners   Sagaponac House 6   3,600 sq ft

Coco Brown suggested in July 2002 the idea of designing the house from the inside out, making the kitchen the center and designing the rest of the house around this core. The proposal shows the integration of the expertise acquired by the design team in the fields of industrial and interior design. A perimeter wall defines the inhabited portion of the site by bending around the house with a variety of earth movements. The level of the terrain rises and drops with varying degrees of privacy afforded to different areas of the house.

The public rooms and the entrance pathway are organized on the ground floor around a small central courtyard. The barrier between living spaces and the courtyard is made of wood panels alternating with glass where natural light is required, such as in the kitchen and the entrance lounge.

The entrance lounge overlooks the pool and the outdoor terrace, which is situated approximately two feet below grade and functions as the domesticated portion of the garden. The second floor houses three bedrooms and a guest room, all facing the sunken pool or the garden that is planted on the roof of the garage.

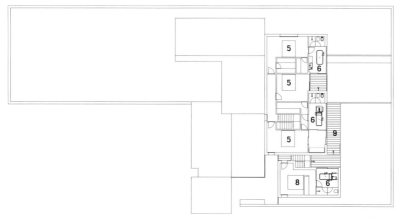

Second Floor

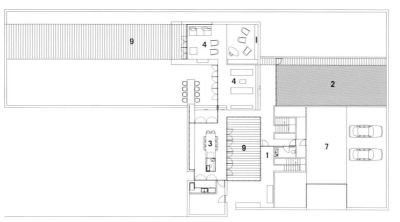

First Floor

1 entrance
2 pool
3 kitchen/dining room
4 living
5 bedroom
6 bathroom
7 garage
8 guest
9 terrace

ABOVE rear elevation
OPPOSITE floor plans

ABOVE kitchen perspective
BELOW sectional perspective

ABOVE perspective of entrance patio
RIGHT guest bathroom

Henry N. Cobb

Pei Cobb Freed & Partners Architects LLP   Sagaponac House 7   3,600 sq ft

Sited in the center of a densely wooded 1.3-acre lot, this one-story house offers a secluded retreat where building and landscape coalesce to achieve a restorative tranquility. The house is composed of two separate pavilions: a living/dining hall with flanking bedroom suites, and a studio with adjacent service spaces. Both pavilions adjoin a garden court whose circumambient porch provides a screened and sheltered walkway between them.

End walls washed with daylight from above dramatize the length and height of the living/dining hall while assuring privacy to the bedroom suites beyond. Along one side of this space, glass-walled galleries flanking a central fireplace open onto a broad veranda that overlooks a lawn and swimming pool nestled in the surrounding forest. Along the opposite side, kitchen and library alcoves flank a large square window, located directly across from the fireplace, with a view into the garden court. Thus, the living/dining hall stands between two realms, inviting its occupants to find pleasure in both: on one side, the social realm of the lawn and swimming pool; on the other, the contemplative realm of the garden court.

The clerestory-lit studio, in contrast, belongs unambiguously to the realm of contemplation. The large cubic volume enclosing this spacious workroom—designed for an artist, writer, or composer—encroaches boldly on the garden court, interrupting its circular berm and ring of flowering trees and giving a glimpse through a corner window into its bowl-shaped center. Here, then, within the confines of a modest weekend house, one encounters an unexpected intimation of limitless space.

Walls and ceilings of the wood-framed house are surfaced with tongue-and-groove cedar boards, painted on the interior and finished with a clear sealer (applied after weathering) on the exterior. Window and door frames are teak, as are floors and decks throughout.

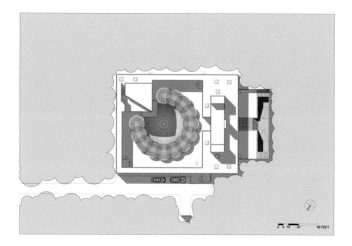

LEFT site plan
OPPOSITE elevation

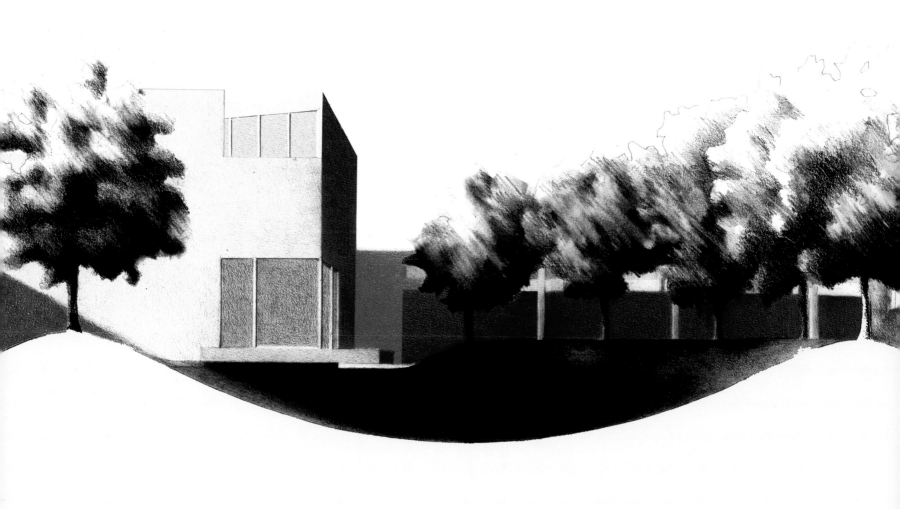

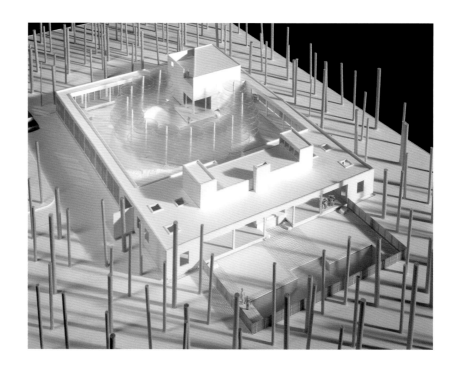

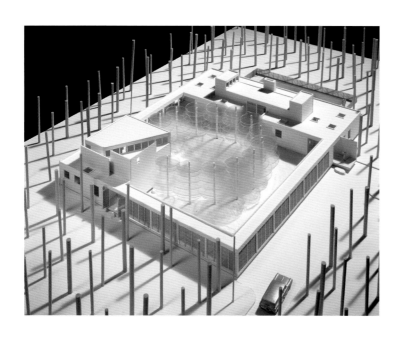

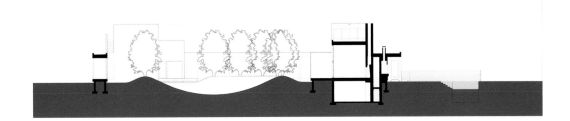

RIGHT section
BELOW floor plan
OPPOSITE models

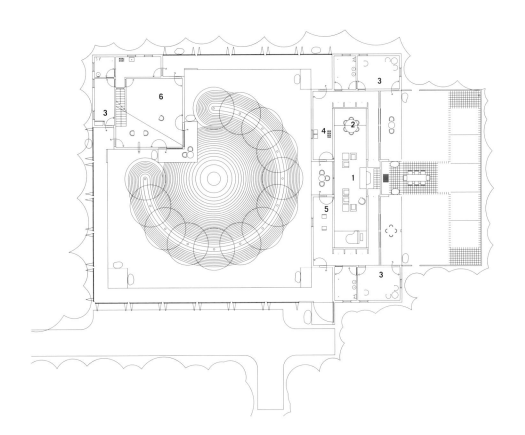

1 living room
2 dining room
3 bedroom
4 kitchen
5 study
6 studio

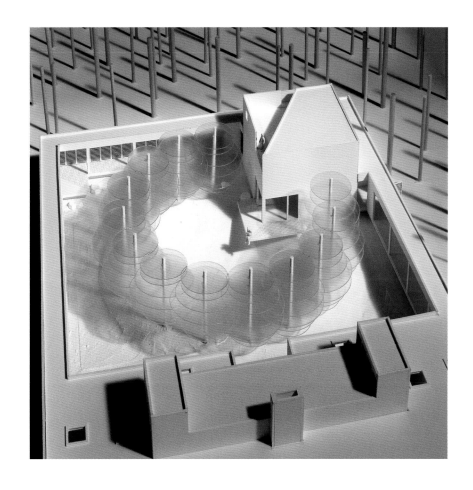

ABOVE model
OPPOSITE interior perspective

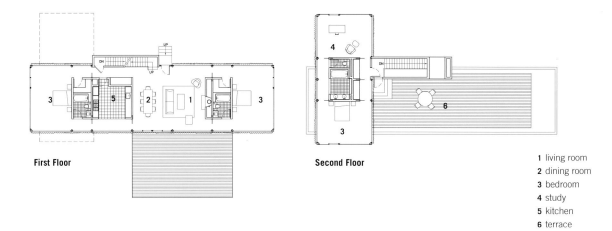

First Floor   **Second Floor**

1 living room
2 dining room
3 bedroom
4 study
5 kitchen
6 terrace

Francois de Menil

Francois de Menil Architect, PC   Sagaponac House 8   3,600 sq ft

"The act of seeing is discontinuous . . . we see only things we are interested in seeing."
                                                              —Paul Nouge

Sagaponac House 8, or the Bikini House, evokes both the iconography of the beach house and the suburban subdivision, examining the perceptions and realities, views and visions of how one lives at leisure and in a community. The house is a "split-level" transparent glass and steel structure that is veiled on the exterior of its long sides with a tightly woven stainless steel mesh curtain. Transparency and views on the short sides are controlled by interior shades. Manipulation of the exterior and interior curtains allows for multiple interpretations of use and program. Only the vertical circulation element is opaque.

The Bikini House is clad with an automated moiré that effectively hides its wholeness while also, at times, obliterating its innocence. The house is comprised of two volumes stacked one upon the other with the upper volume perpendicular to the lower and cantilevered off one end. The two levels are organized around a central core. On the first floor, a living/dining room is flanked by a bedroom and bath at each end. The second floor has a master bedroom with central bath and dressing room. This grid-based plan dissolves in elevation, so that what seems whole in the diagram is actually fragmented in one's selective perception of its three-dimensional form.

ABOVE floor plans
OPPOSITE exterior perspective

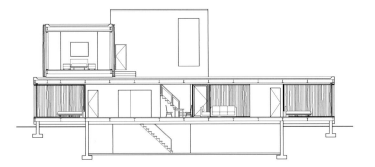

ABOVE conceptual exterior view
LEFT section

ABOVE site plan
RIGHT elevation collage

JAMES INGO FREED

Pei Cobb Freed & Partners Architects, LLP   Sagaponac House 9   3,700 sq ft

Sagaponac House 9 is located approximately in the middle of its site, where it is both a marker and a pivot. The ground is in some places partially displaced so that three occupied floors can be built above it. As a pivot the house accepts deep slices from the entrance point and returns them to a new level, providing entrance to the lowest floor.

The occupied floors from the bottom up start with a kitchen and dining room. On the next level are the main living spaces, which may also be approached from the ground at the entry. The guest bedroom is also on this level. The upper level is the main bedroom suite and small study. An outlying studio at the base level completes the array of spaces.

The house started as an investigation into the possibility of modifying the basic, double overlapping square-rectangle. This aspect of the house required that the stairs be additive to the basic form. Because of the limit to the horizontal dimension where the stairs could fit, their length was accommodated by bending the staircase outwards. These connections were then covered with a metal skin. The library and second bedroom fits into a round two-story element that is also additive to the basic form and therefore clad with the same metal. The kitchen, which occurs between levels one and two, fits the profile of the bent staircase. The rest of the exterior of the house with the exception of the vault surface (which is also metal) is painted white.

Double exposures on the main first and second-level rooms catch and traplight and provide an internal shading zone. Both floors face the pool and its decks. The sloping berms of grass surround this "amusement center" as well as the small pavilion in the garden, providing privacy.

The bedroom suite—all that remains of the eroded second square—opens up and out to views, making it a peaceful, secluded place. The suite is covered by a full-length vault and can access the small balcony on the long side of the house. It is a special space floating to the side of and above the other two floors.

LEFT view from the southeast
OPPOSITE poolside view

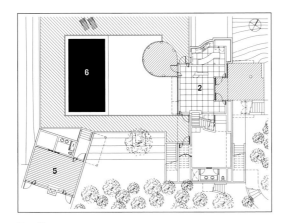

First Floor

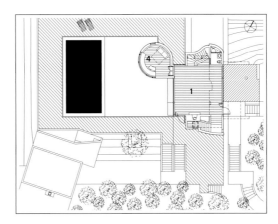

Second Floor

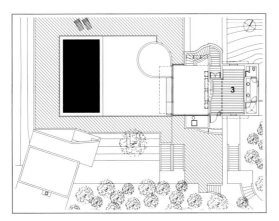

Third Floor

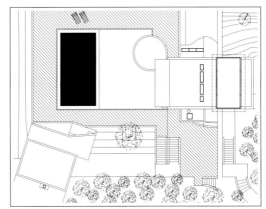

Roof

1 living room
2 dining room/kitchen
3 bedroom
4 study/bedroom
5 studio
6 pool

ABOVE floor plans and roof plan
OPPOSITE view of passage

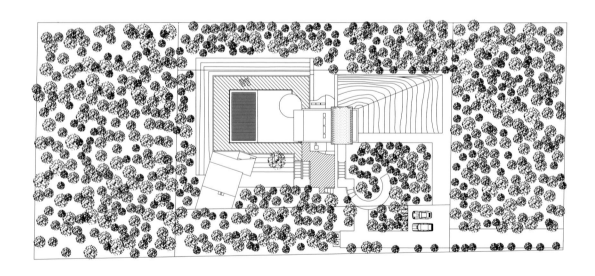

ABOVE concept sketches, site plan
OPPOSITE view of poolside terrace

RICHARD GLUCKMAN

Gluckman Mayner Architects   Sagaponac House 10   3,600 sq ft

In the spirit of a weekend retreat, Sagaponac House 10 optimizes the relationship of interior and exterior spaces. Within the simple box envelope, modest interior living spaces are wrapped by a generous balcony at the southwest corner of both floors. The house is oriented along the cardinal point axes with approach and views directed along the north-south axis, defined as dynamic movement. This action is balanced by the static quality of rooms organized enfilade along the longer east-west axis.

The north and south elevations are clad with sliding wooden slat screen panels configured to modulate the summer sun and breezes. The slats can be adjusted to provide shade to interior spaces and the pool deck as needed. On the second floor the slats are fixed, wood-siding louvers detailed according to solar exposure. Articulation of the extension of this box was determined through the process of formal extraction. Volumes are pulled out of the box to form site elements that are proportionally related to the main house. The entry trellis and dining deck are extruded from the living space centered around the kitchen as the garage links back to the vertical stair volume. The pool mirrors the living room in plan and reflects afternoon sun onto its ceiling.

The interior is organized around two solid stacked service cores consisting of the kitchen and bathrooms. The master bedroom located above the living area has its own terrace; guest/children's bedrooms and bathrooms are designed as flexible spaces with movable walls and sliding doors. Vertical elements along the north facade generate height and volume. The stair and skylight allow light into the house and reinforce the openness of the interior spaces.

The economy of this simple layout organizes the program requirements within a rigid frame. An economy of means generates an economy of form. Inexpensive mass-produced manufactured materials such as polycarbonate glazing, cement board siding, and engineered lumber framing contribute to the efficient, spare simplicity of this weekend retreat.

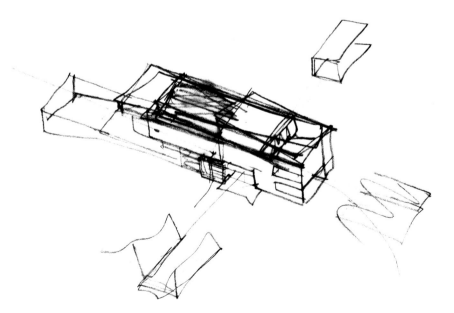

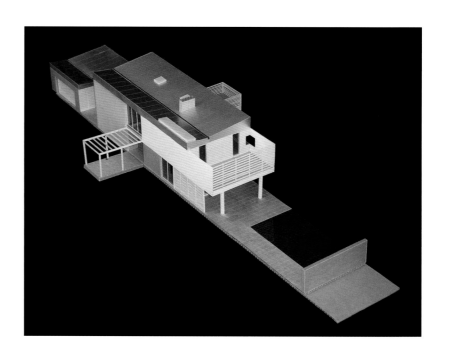

North elevation

South elevation

ABOVE model, aerial view of northwest corner
LEFT elevations
OPPOSITE (top) schematic volumetric study
OPPOSITE (bottom) northeast entry perspective

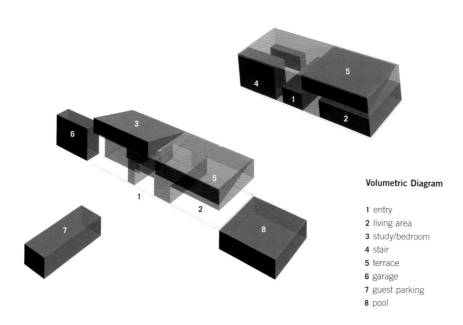

Volumetric Diagram

1 entry
2 living area
3 study/bedroom
4 stair
5 terrace
6 garage
7 guest parking
8 pool

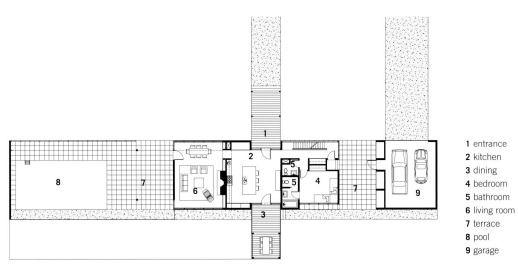

First Floor

1 entrance
2 kitchen
3 dining
4 bedroom
5 bathroom
6 living room
7 terrace
8 pool
9 garage

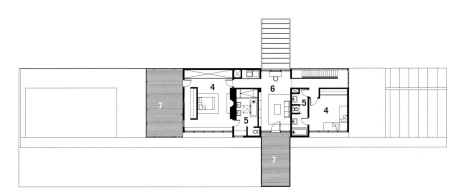

Second Floor

ABOVE floor plans
RIGHT cross section
OPPOSITE perspective from pool

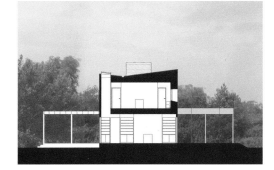

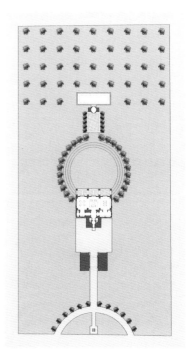

Michael Graves

Michael Graves & Associates   Sagaponac House 11   3,300 sq ft

Michael Graves's program for Sagaponac House 11 includes a living room, dining room, library, kitchen, and two bedrooms in the main house, with options for a studio and a one- or two-car garage. These three components form a central courtyard that creates a sense of arrival and provides privacy for the house.

Aligned with the driveway's axis, a tower with canted walls marks the entrance to the house and contains a staircase that spirals around a three-story cylinder, capped with an oculus that allows light to filter into the vestibule. The tower terminates in a roof terrace over the full extent of the footprint of the house, with views to the sea beyond.

The house plan is simple and clear. The main living space is a large loft-like room that is subdivided into three discrete spaces (living room, dining room, and library) with individual characters. The double height living room in the center provides privacy between the bedrooms on the floor above. The dining room is adjacent to the kitchen, and the library has access to the bathroom and wet bar. French doors from each of these rooms open to a terrace and pergola overlooking the rear yard.

The rear yard, with its sunken amphitheater, echoes the privacy of the front court. A circle of trees encloses this space, creating, in effect, an outdoor room. A small folly, perhaps a pool house or a gazebo, marks the end of the primary axis.

The exterior materials, stained cedar siding and white wood trim, are typical of Long Island beachfront communities. The siding is laid vertically on the tower to emphasize its height while the house's main volume is clad horizontally in wide bands that provide an unexpected grandness of scale to this small and simple house.

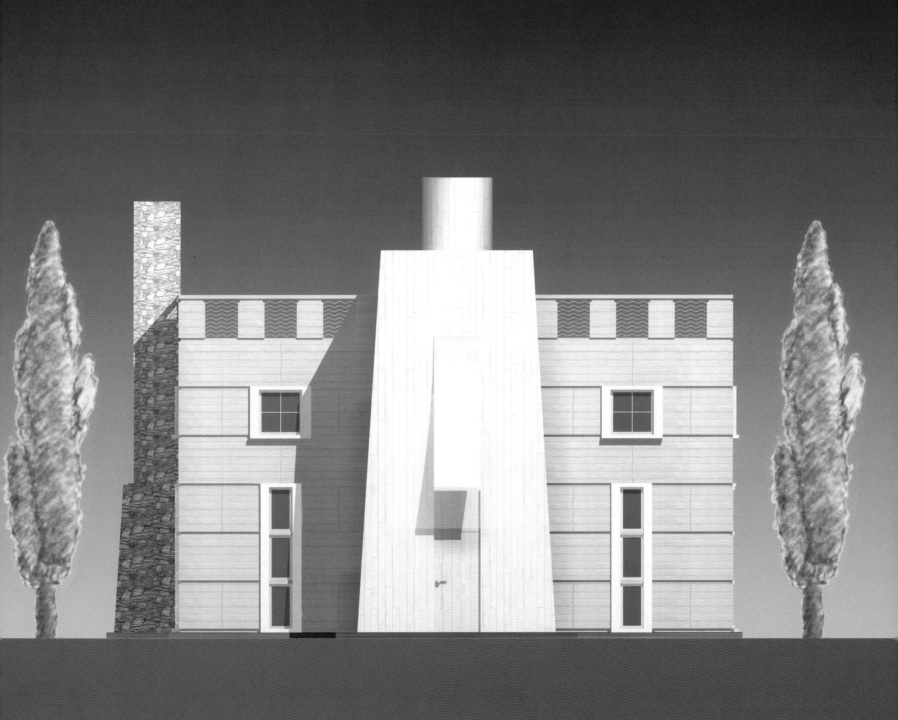

First Floor

Second Floor

1 living room
2 dining room
3 bedroom

ABOVE section, floor plans
OPPOSITE south elevation

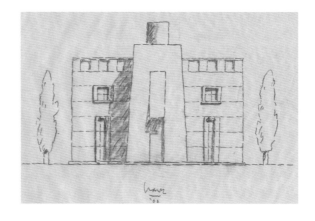

LEFT Michael Graves's design sketches
OPPOSITE north elevation

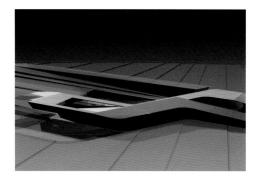

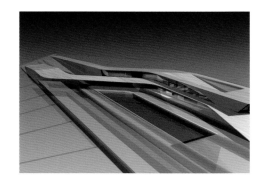

ZAHA HADID

Zaha Hadid Architects   Sagaponac House 12   3,300 sq ft

In Sagaponac House 12, the architect manipulates the ground and articulates structure as a new form of landscape. The idea is to construct or continue the natural site through an artificial landscape formation whereby three concrete bands articulate artificial hills. These landscape analogies result in open, fluid and flexible floorplans.

The organization of the plan is critical and implies a way for inhabitants to move through the site. An elevated path runs over the building and cuts through it as well. The ground is lifted as a floor slab, which is then cut and peeled back to bring light into the space below. Parts of the interior of the building are externalized; building and landscape merge.

The natural site is carved away to prepare a field for the incision of the project. The ground is articulated as a layered topography by peeling, warping and multiplying the site surface. The ground condition operates on the oblique, starting at street level with zero and then gently moving both up and down. Three masses are created which utilize large parcels of the site and transform them into new building features: the main space, guest area and pool. The plan enables a juxtaposition of various events, which are embedded in the building's internal spatial system.

The architectural experience begins at the north entrance of the site. The street is extended into the landscape to lead visitors to the garage in the right wing of the building. This area also contains two bedrooms for guests or family. The entry path further continues to the left side into the main building. A spacious open passage leads to the living area, which opens its south facade to the exterior and pool. The space extends upward to the master bedroom on the second level, which offers a generous view across the site. This area further folds onto the roof terrace, which is fully accessible and allows a gentle descent back to the main site entrance.

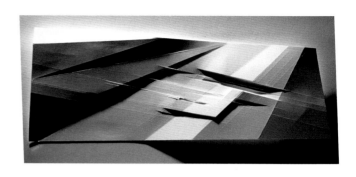

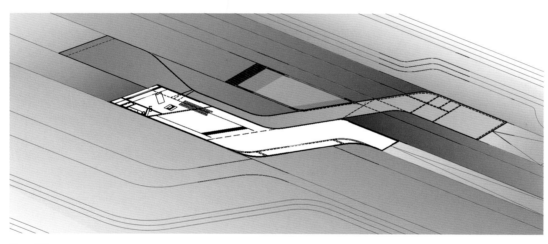

Second Floor

1 main entrance
2 kitchen
3 reception
4 living room
5 bedroom
6 bathroom
7 pool
8 garage

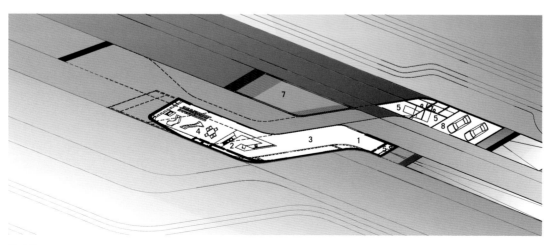

First Floor

ABOVE study model
LEFT floor plans
OPPOSITE poolside view

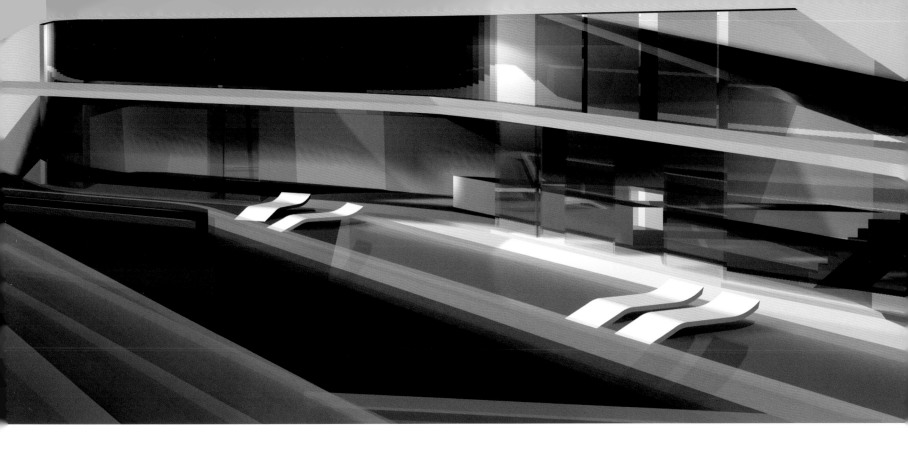

Thomas Hanrahan & Victoria Meyers

Hanrahan Meyers Architects   Sagaponac House 13   3,400 sq ft

Sagaponac House 13 is a four-bedroom courtyard house that is a "sculpture for living in," full of unexpected views and spaces. A transparent lower level enclosed by frameless glass connects the surrounding Long Island landscape of grasses to the ground-floor spaces. Materials are natural and elegant, and include wood clapboard with glass and wood windows, maple plank floors, plaster walls, and stone details such as kitchen and bath counters and the fireplace mantel. The natural surroundings flow into and through the house—from the grass of the surrounding site, to the wood planks of the deck, and the wood of the floors in the house—to form a unified living environment.

First Floor

Second Floor

1 entrance
2 kitchen
3 dining room
4 living room
5 bedroom
6 bathroom
7 guest
8 carport
9 terrace

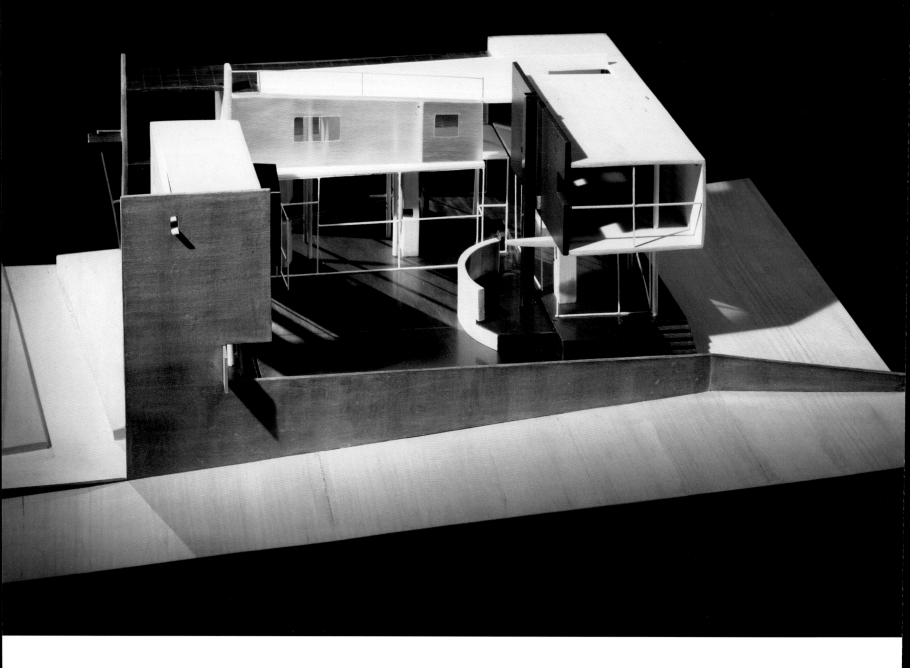

RIGHT view from entry
BELOW view from terrace
OPPOSITE model, courtyard view

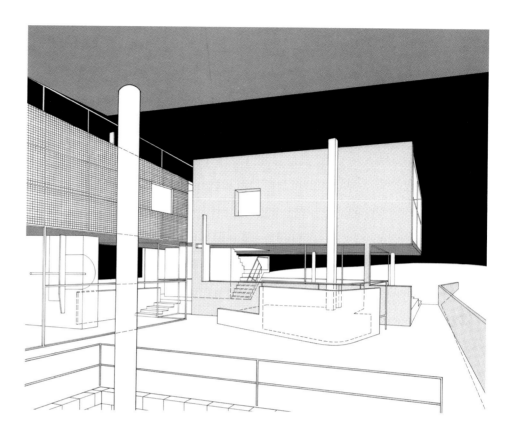

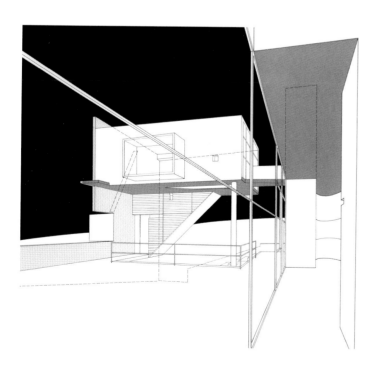

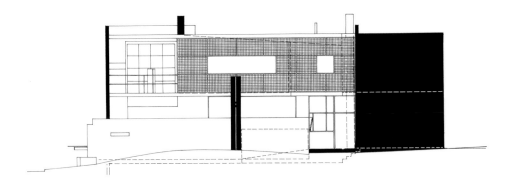

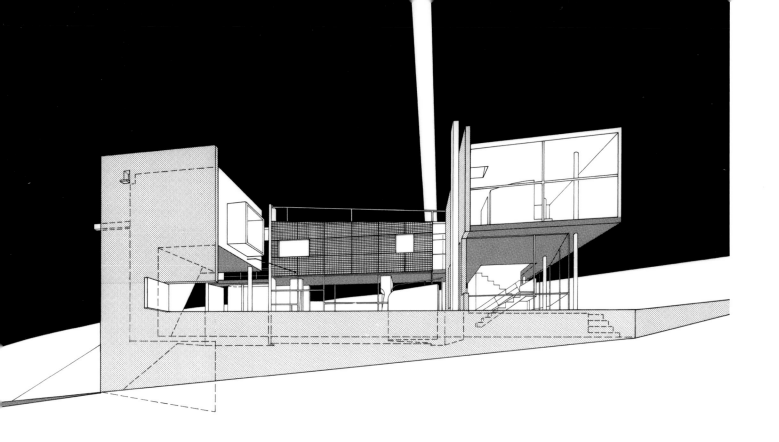

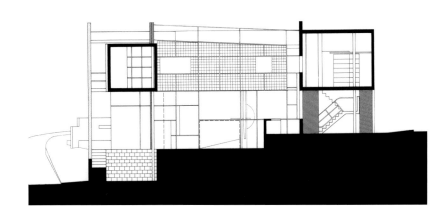

ABOVE view looking into courtyard
RIGHT section through courtyard

GISUE HARIRI & MOJGAN HARIRI

Hariri & Hariri - Architecture   Sagaponac House 14   5,000 sq ft

Inspired by Alberto Giacometti's sculpture titled Figure in a Box between Two Boxes which are Houses, Sagaponac House 14 takes the form of a minimalist structure placed on a platform within the untouched natural landscape. The spatial configuration of the house invites variety of personalities and occupants, from hermetic individuals to sociable couples or groups, to be "original" and invent their own way of habitation in this structure.

Composed of two simple rectangular volumes forming an L-Shaped plan, the house engages the landscape and the pleasures of being in the country by framing it. The center of the house is the main public space with a swimming pool, multilevel terraces, and a covered porch with a shower. This space, accessible and visible to all other parts of the house, and at times visible to the neighbors and the street, becomes a stage for action and display.

A large opening within each rectangular volume frames the private life of the house and the pool. These openings appear and disappear via a system of metal shutters mounted on the exterior walls. The metal shutters not only act as a shield against intruders when no one is at home, they also reveal and conceal private and public hidden motivations, social interaction, and exchanges within and beyond the house.

OPPOSITE (top) site model

OPPOSITE (bottom) Giacometti sculpture
(*Alberto Giacometti* published by the Museum of Modern Art
and the Kunsthaus, Zurich, in 2001. Photographer: Ernst Scheidegger.)

BELOW entrance view

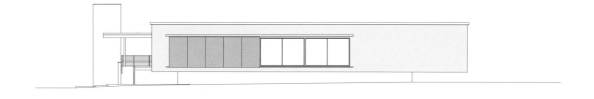

ABOVE north elevation, east elevation
RIGHT floor plan
BELOW sketches
OPPOSITE poolside view

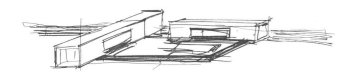

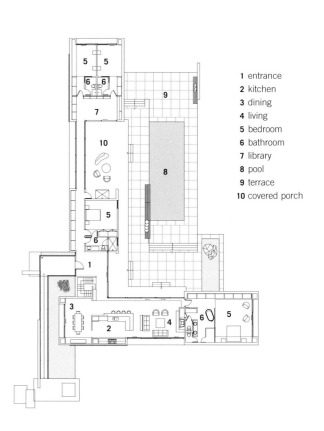

1 entrance
2 kitchen
3 dining
4 living
5 bedroom
6 bathroom
7 library
8 pool
9 terrace
10 covered porch

ABOVE interior view of living room
OPPOSITE (top) view of covered porch and glazed passerelle
OPPOSITE (bottom) covered porch and outdoor terraces

STEVEN HARRIS

Steven Harris Architects   Sagaponac House 15   3,200 sq ft

Two distinct volumes of Sagaponac House 15, which architect Steven Harris has dubbed "The Loft and the Motel," intersect at a screened porch that filters movement from the outside in and from the "loft" to the "motel." At once a glass box and a dormitory, this house conjures different notions of domestic life, comfortably allowing for both private and public living. Built of structurally insulated panels and sheathed in cedar, the "motel" is an efficient two-story volume of bedrooms, bathrooms, and garage. Light enters through horizontal slots on the ground floor and skylights and light monitors on the upper floor.

The "loft," by comparison, offers views out to the densely forested site. The space accomodates large gatherings but also encourages intimacy. Two hearths organize the space and serve as anchoring points: one in the kitchen, and another straddling the glass enclosure and screened porch. A landscaped roof provides sound insulation.

The architect has planned several measures to make the house ecologically and thermally efficient: passive cooling (including ground cooling, earth ducting, and natural ventilation), water recycling (rainwater and graywater), structurally insulated wall panels, and a "vegetated" roof. These features lower energy costs and connect the house to the site in a direct and sustainable manner.

ABOVE site plan
OPPOSITE north elevation

ABOVE west elevation
BELOW floor plans

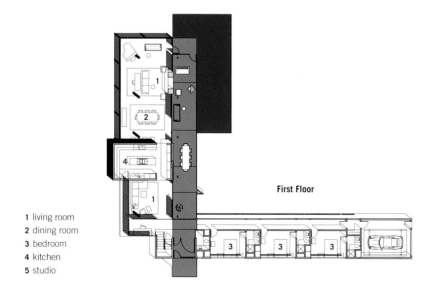

1 living room
2 dining room
3 bedroom
4 kitchen
5 studio

First Floor

Second Floor

ABOVE interior perspective
RIGHT exterior perspective

CRAIG HODGETTS & HSIN-MING FUNG

Hodgetts + Fung   Sagaponac House 16   4,300 sq ft

Craig Hodgetts and Hsin-ming Fung designed Sagaponac House 16 to inject the feel of Southern California into the social and environmental climate of Sagaponac. The individual rooms and spaces of the house are arranged informally around a glass-enclosed courtyard, which forms a cubelike volume designed to capture fragments of the surrounding rooms, spaces, and landscape. The resulting three-dimensional array confers order on an otherwise spontaneous composition, somewhat like the framing device of a photographer's lens. This living volume functions as a shelter under which the active elements of the program are arranged, producing a dynamic living environment that is also casual and intimate, appropriate to a family that enjoys opening its home to guests. Perhaps the signature feature of the house is the retractable wall of glass that rises into a glass case viewable above the roof, separating the cubic volume of the ground floor from the yard.

The second floor, a large, family-sized kitchen, acts as a hub for activity in the home, linking a home office, master bedroom suite, dining balcony, and panoramic living room to a grand stair ascending from the "virtual" space of the ground floor. The continuity of defining surfaces encourages the flow of indoor to outdoor space, extending occupants' sightlines into the landscaped grounds, where echoes of the governing geometry are seen.

ABOVE axonometric illustration
OPPOSITE southwest view

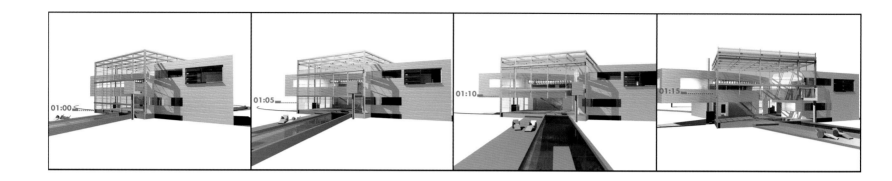

ABOVE animated frames showing operation of atrium wall
BELOW west elevation

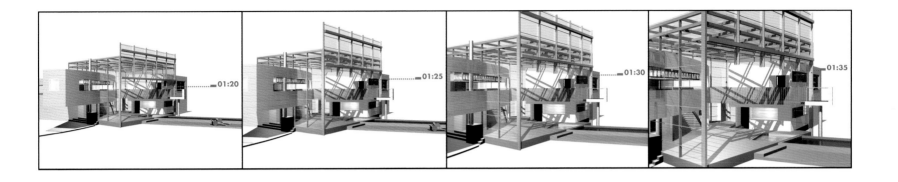

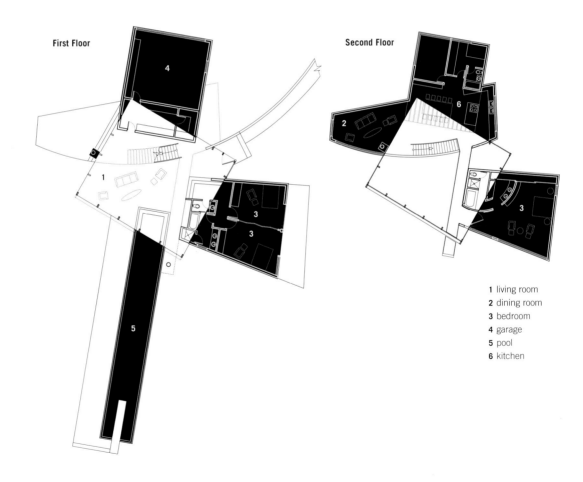

First Floor

Second Floor

1 living room
2 dining room
3 bedroom
4 garage
5 pool
6 kitchen

RIGHT floor plans

ABOVE hot tub under moonlight
OPPOSITE interior perspective

STEVEN HOLL

Steven Holl Architects   Sagaponac House 17   2,500 sq ft

A T-shaped pool joins together the powerful triad of sculptural forms that comprises Sagaponac House 17. This pool is imagined as the base of a tube of space pushing through three rectangles. Each perspective dissolves in the landscape outside the plan as the shaft of space cuts through a concrete block prism. The largest prism contains a loftlike living/dining area overlooked by a large bedroom, while the second prism contains two bedrooms over a recreation area. The smallest prism holds an art studio located above a carport. A secret gallery illuminated by skylights under twelve feet of water connects the house and guest house.

Solar stack walls of channel glass and ducted air cavities are found on each south-facing elevation, providing sixty percent of the domestic heat and, due to chimney effect, evaporative cooling in the summer. Interior materials consist of integral color concrete floors and bamboo wood cabinets and doors. The roofs are planted green in two feet of sedum, a special short-length sod.

Movement and spatial perspective overlap from the moment of arrival in the carport, where an open view down the water channel unfolds. One walks along the poolside to enter the main house through a single glass door that opens to the dining/living space. A wide stair leads down to the passage below the pool. Large enough for game tables, the long space rises at the far end in a stair leading to a recreation room. Space shaped by simple volumes, rather than objective form, casts the larger aim of this villa as an argument for nature conservation and urban consolidation.

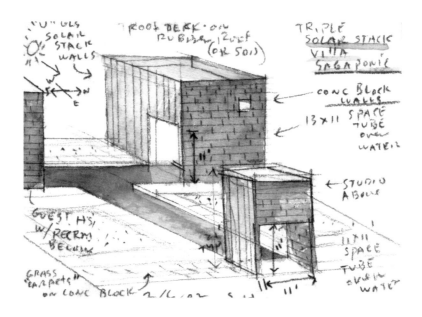

ABOVE courtyard perspective, T-shaped pool connecting building volumes
BELOW floor plans
OPPOSITE early sketch

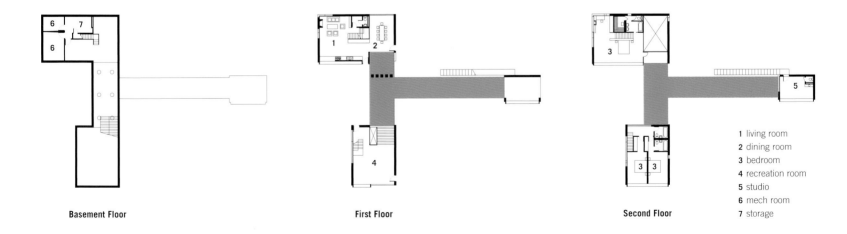

Basement Floor

First Floor

Second Floor

1 living room
2 dining room
3 bedroom
4 recreation room
5 studio
6 mech room
7 storage

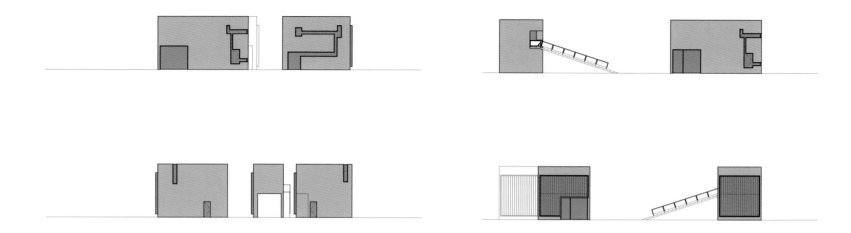

ABOVE elevations
LEFT exterior perspective of main house

SAND RECTANGLE
NORTH ELV. TRIPLE VILLA / SAGA PONIC

ABOVE initial sketch
RIGHT north elevation

119

CARLOS JIMENEZ

Carlos Jimenez Studio   Sagaponac House 18   3,100 sq ft

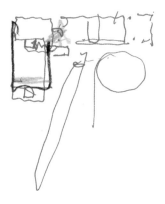

The 3,100-square-foot, two-story Sagaponac House 18 is an L-shaped volume inserted in a predominantly wooded site. The public spaces, which comprise living, dining, study, and kitchen, are located on the ground floor. A common entryway links the two wings of the house and provides access to outside gardens. The gardens can also be reached from the open carport, which also functions as a large outdoor room. The second floor contains two bedrooms, the main bedroom, and bathrooms. Echoing the potential of the carport as outside room, an upper deck and overhead trellis is located directly above the garage. The deck offers expansive views of the surrounding landscape and grounds.

The two wings of the house allow for a clear separation of program without compromising the integrity of the house as a whole. The house's primary quality is its generous allocation of natural light, carefully diffused throughout the interior spaces to avoid unnecessary heat gain and glare in the summer months. The wood-framed structure is clad in stained cypress siding and stucco painted a vibrant green. Minimal and precise details in the interior spaces contribute to the house's spare luxury.

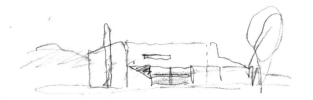

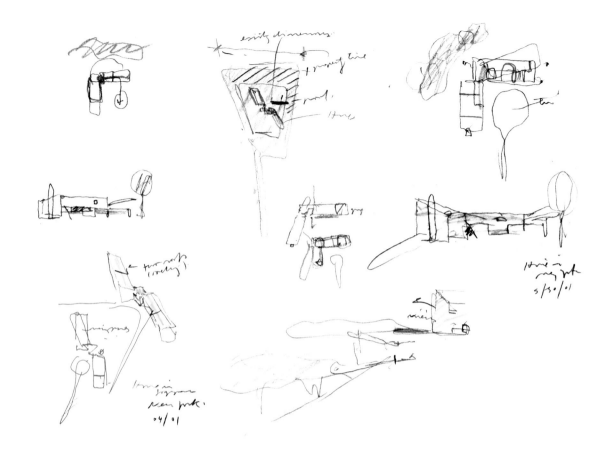

First Floor

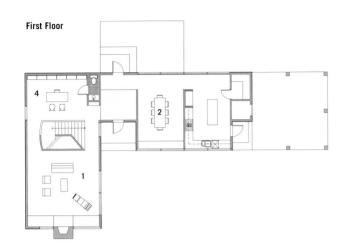

Second Floor

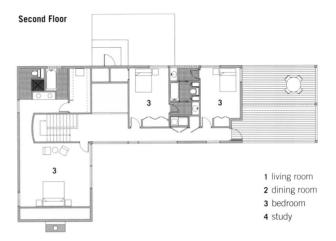

1 living room
2 dining room
3 bedroom
4 study

ABOVE floor plans
RIGHT concept sketches

PHILIP JOHNSON & ALAN RITCHIE

Philip Johnson/Alan Ritchie Architects   Sagaponac House 19   2,900 sq ft

Philip Johnson has often delighted in designing new buildings based on older ones. For Sagaponac House 19, Philip Johnson and his partner, Alan Ritchie, underscore this desire to make new structures recognizable as descendants of historic architecture.

Here, they have selected none other than the Pantheon in Rome as inspiration for domestic architecture. The famous dome's silhouette is quoted nearly verbatim, but unlike the original, Johnson and Ritchie's version appears in multiples. The Pantheon has become a module, a building block. These domes are clustered like a village and appear in different scales.

Once the building block was chosen, Johnson and Ritchie made numerous studies before deciding to arrange these objects as a series of clusters. Johnson and Ritchie were particularly engaged by the possibility of creating a village out of a series of domed rooms, as well as by the effect of scale on a form well known for its fixed proportions. It is extraordinary how adding a few feet to the diameter of any of these rooms creates a completely different sense of space. This, of course, provided the opportunity to create a variety of combinations of large and small rooms. The functions of these rooms skillfully supplement one other.

While it may seem ironic to select a building as civic and solemn as the Pantheon for a house project, this hardly unsettles Johnson, who sees it as a terrific opportunity to blend the grand tradition of architectural history with the design of a house.

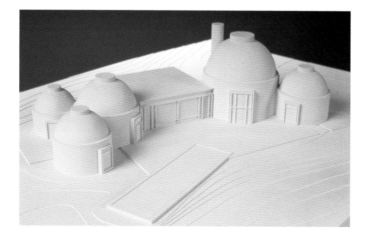

LEFT model
OPPOSITE entry perspective

RIGHT west, north and south elevations
BELOW site map
OPPOSITE southeast perspective
OVERLEAF east elevation

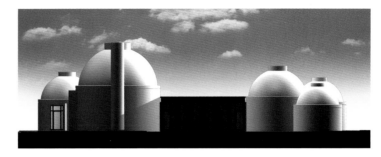

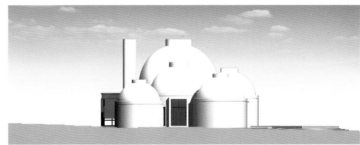

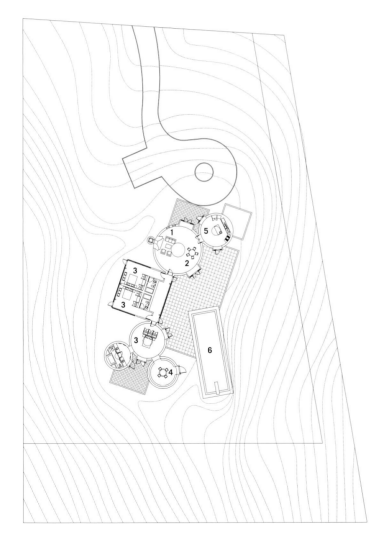

1 living room
2 dining room
3 bedroom
4 study
5 kitchen
6 pool

127

ROBERT KAHN

Robert Kahn Architect   Sagaponac House 20   2,300 sq ft

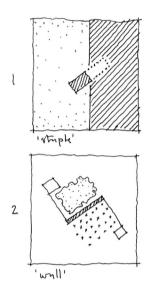

The main house is 1,800 square feet with a 300-square-foot garage/studio and a 200-square-foot pool house. The main house is divided into two parts: one "open," the other "solid." The open half is a double-height, glass-enclosed living/dining room. The solid half contains two floors, the first of which consists of an entry, kitchen, bath, and bedroom (convertible to two bedrooms). The second floor is dedicated to the master bedroom suite and includes a sitting room/study that overlooks the living room. From this balcony an exterior stair leads to a roof garden with a pavilion that is itself divided into two parts: a screened sleeping porch and a covered open porch. The roof garden also contains an exterior fireplace and hot tub. A ship's ladder leads to a widow's walk on the roof of the pavilion, affording views to the ocean.

The main house is an elongated rectangle that acts as a "staple" between the wooded landscape and a manicured clearing; the open glass living room sits in the woods, the solid half of the house sits in the clearing. The pool house and garage are set away from the main house at opposite ends and on opposite sides, each with its own private garden. The main house functions as a wall between the pool house and the garage/studio.

ABOVE Conceptual sketch, 'staple' and 'wall'

130

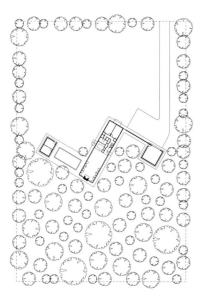

ABOVE perspective from rear yard
LEFT site plan

ABOVE poolside perspective
OPPOSITE floor and roof plans

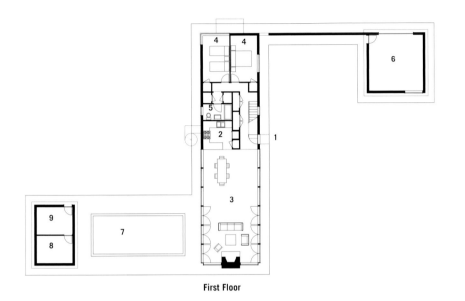

First Floor

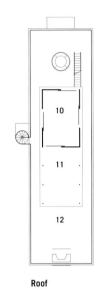

Roof

1 entrance
2 kitchen
3 living/dining room
4 bedroom
5 bathroom
6 garage/studio
7 pool
8 sauna
9 changing room
10 sleeping porch
11 covered terrace
12 roof terrace
13 widow's walk

open to below

Second Floor

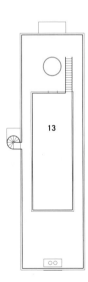

Upper Roof

133

STEPHEN H. KANNER

Kanner Architects   Sagaponac House 21   3,600 sq ft

Honored with the American Institute of Architects' Next LA Award, Sagaponac House 21 is the product of the development's mission of "modesty of scale and economics" that respects and celebrates, through design, the natural setting. The architect's solution includes raising the house on a two-foot-high wooden plinth. The budget necessitated a simple partie: a 20-foot-wide double rectangle plan form connected by a glass-clad hall surrounding a central courtyard. The narrow width of the rectangular volumes economizes on structural costs through repetition of beam and joist sizes while providing openness and views along both longitudinal elevations.

The two-story volume is wrapped in a reddish/orange stained cedar ribbon that pays homage to the spectacular fall colors of New England. On the lower floor, living room, dining room, and kitchen all open to the large surrounding deck via broad sliding doors. The second floor is accessed by either a sculptural stair that wraps around the two-story living room's fireplace or by a secondary spiral stair. This level has three bedrooms, each with a wide balcony.

Argon-filled dual glazed windows guard against heat gain and loss. Rooms are easily cross-ventilated due to the structure's narrow width and multiple sliding doors. Materials are few and restrained: wooden floors, steel and glass window walls, gypsum board and cedar paneled walls, a concrete fireplace, glass railings, Douglas fir cabinets with stainless steel tops, and statuary marble in the bathrooms.

The project's design is minimalist, almost a mirror of the forest it sits within. If it were to visually disappear, the architect's ultimate goal would be met: a reflection of nature. For the inhabitants, though, the mission was to eliminate the distinction between interior and exterior space, so all can be viewed without interruption.

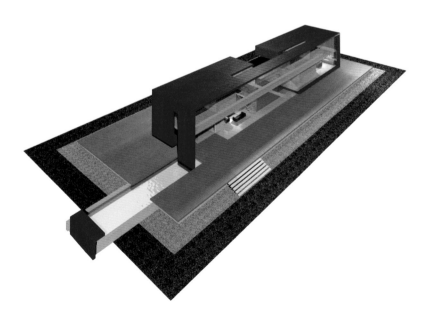

LEFT aerial perspective
OPPOSITE exterior perspective, living room

First Floor

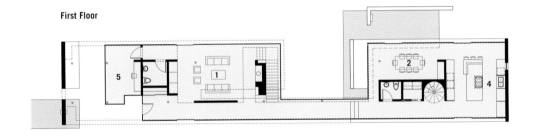

ABOVE sectional perspective
LEFT floor plans

Second Floor

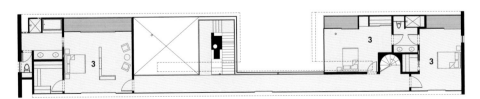

1 living room
2 dining room
3 bedroom
4 kitchen
5 study

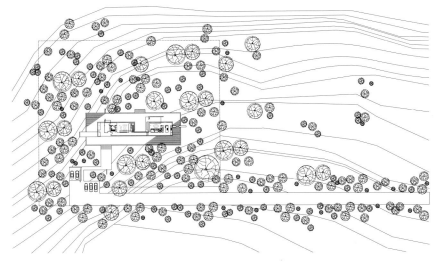

ABOVE exterior perspective, kitchen and dining room
RIGHT site plan
OVERLEAF north perspective at night

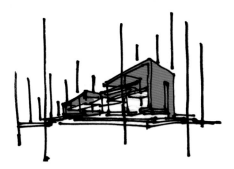

JOHN KEENEN & TERENCE RILEY

Keenen/Riley (K/R)   Sagaponac House 22   3,000 sq ft

Sagaponac House 22, or the Split House, is designed to accommodate different patterns of contemporary domesticity simultaneously: solitude, work, interaction, and relaxation. Family, guests, and friends, in whatever combination, freely activate the loosely structured house. The main space in the house is the terrace between the two principle volumes of the house, both of which are two stories. The lower level of the structure to the right of the entry steps—containing the garage, a solarium, and outdoor shower—is tucked under the upper-level bedroom and an artist's studio adjacent to a swimming pool. Opposite, two additional bedrooms occupy the upper level of the second structure, with the main social spaces—kitchen/dining room, living room, screened porch—below. To keep the experience fluid, the "in-between" character of the terrace is repeated on a mezzanine level off the stair of the main house. This mid-level space straddles the private and social realms of the house, and provides respite from the main activities of the house. The windows of this room capture the north light, and open onto a grove of bamboo.

The house is simply constructed using common materials: wood and steel framing, cement block and stucco walls, and clear wood siding on the upper levels. The house volumes are given generous terraces, providing each room with direct access to the outdoors. Like the Renaissance double house Villa Lante, the emptiness at the center of the house keeps activity—in short, living—as the focus of the house. The raised terrace encourages the use of outdoor space for everything from cooking and dining to sunning and relaxing.

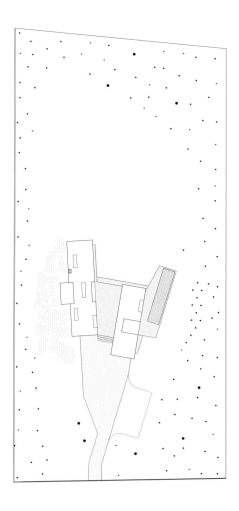

ABOVE view from poolside
OPPOSITE site plan

LEFT view of poolhouse
BELOW aerial perspective

RIGHT view of entry and poolhouse
BELOW floor plans

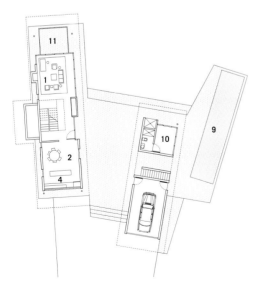

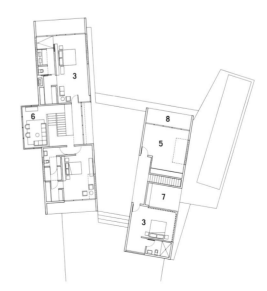

1 living room
2 dining room
3 bedroom
4 kitchen
5 studio
6 sitting room
7 sundeck
8 terrace
9 pool
10 pool room
11 screened porch

First Floor

Second Floor

Samuel Mockbee

Samuel Mockbee Architect   Sagaponac House 24   4,800 sq ft

Sagaponac House 24 makes a clear separation between an open, column-free volume that contains the living/public sections of the house and the closed-off and private bedrooms sheathed in plated, angular metal panels.

The living/public spaces, placed over the service zones of the house, open to the site through a continuous glass wall overlooking the pool. This simple arrangement allows for free-form spaces that offer elevated views of the site. Adjoining the main room are smaller spaces in which to read, nap, or sit by a fire. The focus of the interior living space is the kitchen. Enclosed by a free-form truss roof that allows for clerestory windows around the perimeter, this amorphous part of the house is grounded to the site by stairs and terraces.

To complete the house, an elevated screen porch—a place to socialize and enjoy the outside from within—overlooks the pool and tennis court. The porch is protected by an angular roof similar to the forms at the opposite end of the house, but is also open and inviting; it hangs under the branches suspended on its own structure, blending into the outdoors setting.

ABOVE site plan
OPPOSITE partial section

ABOVE elevation sketch of poolside
BELOW floor plans

First Floor

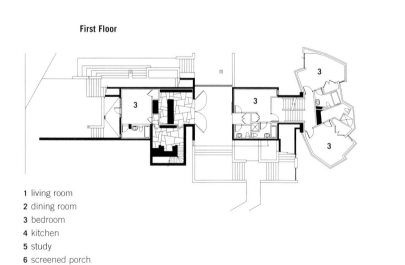

Second Floor

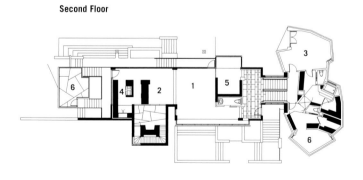

1 living room
2 dining room
3 bedroom
4 kitchen
5 study
6 screened porch

149

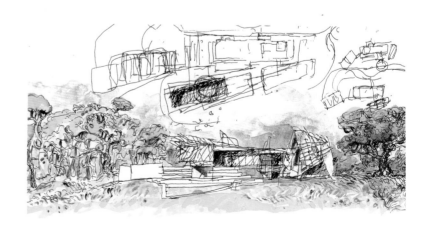

ABOVE and RIGHT initial concept sketches
OPPOSITE elevation sketch

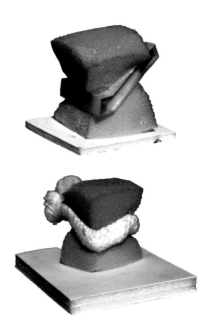

ERIC OWEN MOSS

Eric Owen Moss Architects   Sagaponac House 25   3,700 sq ft

Sagaponac House 25 consists of a main block with a double-height living space, mezzanine, master bedroom, and a wraparound circulation stair, which seems to be squeezing the main block. Adjoined is a secondary one-story block with garage, storage, suite, and kitchen, an exterior patio area for gathering, and a water element, possibly for swimming.

The main block frame consists of three columns and beams; located by a triangle in plan, a secondary steel frame for the stair. The wraparound stair provides floor-to-ceiling glazing continuously from ground level to the top. Walls of the main block are made with ribs to give the exterior curve and interior planar surfaces ease of construction. The space between the walls can be used for mechanical systems, insulation, and so on. Walls of the secondary block are typical wood frame construction. Exterior wood shingles are proposed for the roof and walls to homogenize the house and for ease of construction.

The living room is a double-height space with faceted walls. The mezzanine has a panoramic view of the surrounding landscape. It could be used as a library/study with shelving. Fireplaces are located in the living room and the master bedroom. Typical operable window types are located in rooms for light and air.

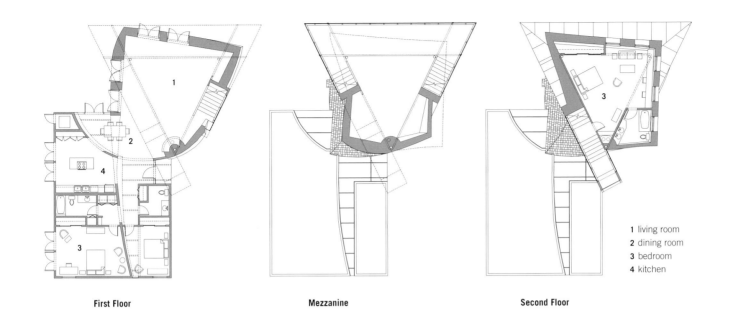

First Floor

Mezzanine

Second Floor

1 living room
2 dining room
3 bedroom
4 kitchen

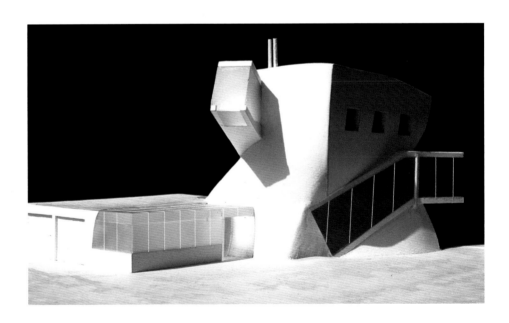

ABOVE floor plans
RIGHT model, south elevation
OPPOSITE southwest elevation

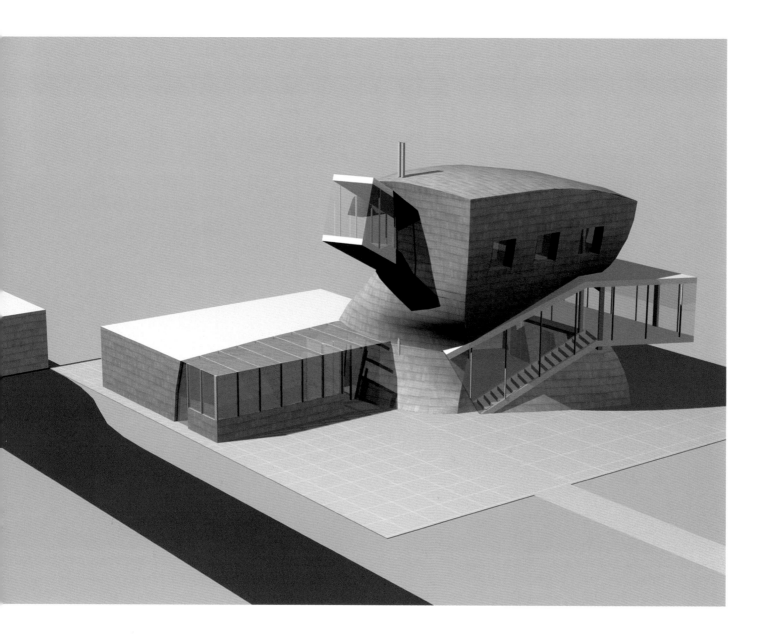

RIGHT conceptual sketch
BELOW structural model
OPPOSITE aerial view looking north
OVERLEAF north elevation

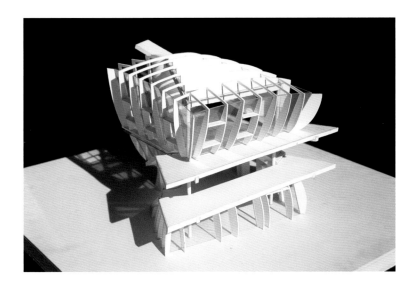

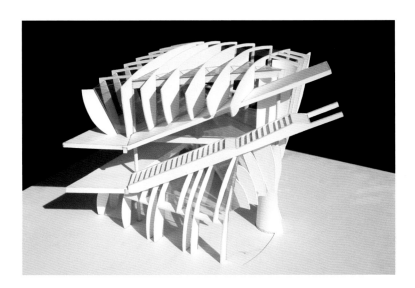

WINY MAAS, JACOB VAN RIJS & NATHALIE DE VRIES

MVRDV   Sagaponac House 26   3,000 sq ft

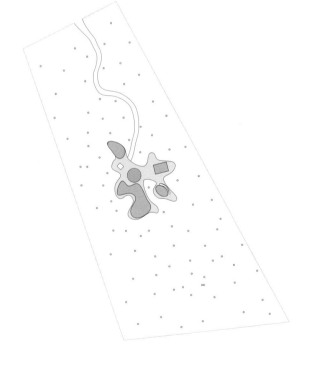

By positioning Sagaponac House 26 at the level of the site's treetops, MVRDV preserves nature and simultaneously provides an escape from it. The house is composed as a sandwich of two decks among the tops of the existing trees. The upper deck is a floating garden with panoramic views over the forest to the ocean. It offers a retreat from the forest and space for the forest to flourish virtually undisturbed. Underneath the sundeck is a lower deck conceived as a giant veranda, where the interior spaces of the house are located and where the forest's foliage become the walls of the house. Three different volumes are situated on the veranda: the living area, the sleeping area, and the pool. These three "huts" provide maximal contact with the surrounding landscape and form a village in the sky.

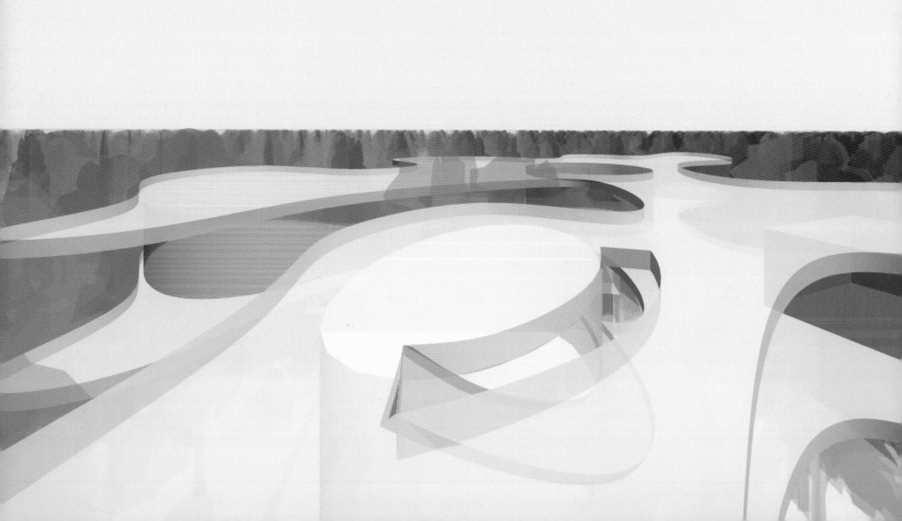

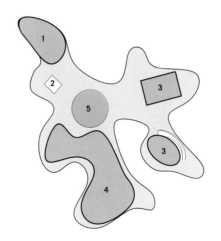

1 parlor
2 elevator
3 bedroom
4 living/dining/kitchen area
5 pool

RIGHT floor plan
ABOVE interior perspective
OPPOSITE rooftop perspective

164

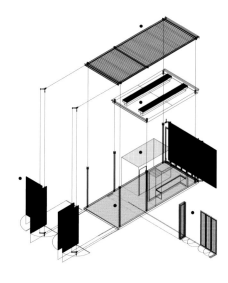

THOMAS PHIFER

Thomas Phifer and Partners   Sagaponac House 27   2,400 sq ft

Sagaponac House 27 is a place of quiet contemplation and a retreat from the cease-less activity inherent in city life. In the residential tradition of eastern Long Island, the protective hedges define the outdoor spaces and bring a human scale to the openness of the landscape. The new horizon defined by the hedges allows for a compositional strategy similar to the Shakkei, or "borrowed landscape," strategy used in Zen gardens, wherein the composition of the foreground is carefully arranged to incorporate views as a visitor moves through the garden.

In the foreground composition, the containment of protective outdoor room acts as a simple backdrop to the careful placement of two simple elements within: the house and the lap pool. The two parallel shade panel walls are designed to keep the enclo-sure cool from the outside and to provide flexible sun control and privacy. These form a permeable surface that define the transition from the landscape to the porch enclosure similar to the organization of a Japanese temple. Above these shade panels is a layer of horizontal louvers that provide shade and filtered light for the porch. Set above the porch, they keep direct sunlight from heating the house during the summer season's intensive solar radiation at a steep sun angle. During winter season, solar radiation at lower angles is permitted through the louvers resulting in desirable solar heat gains.

The house program has been split into enclosures, one containing the living room, dining room, and master bedroom suite, and the other accommodating two guest bed-room suites with a common sitting room. The two enclosures are separated by a breezeway that serves as the main arrival point for the house. The two wings are enclosed by simple, operable folding doors to permit easy access to the porch and an abundance of natural ventilation. The interior partitions are lined with natural wood paneling. From within this evanescent enclosure, framed views to the landscape open through the shade panels, open or closed.

ABOVE exploded view of single bay
OPPOSITE exterior view, screens open

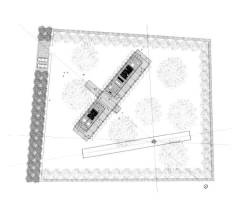

1 living room
2 dining room
3 bedroom

BELOW (top) site plan, floor plan
BELOW (bottom) interior view

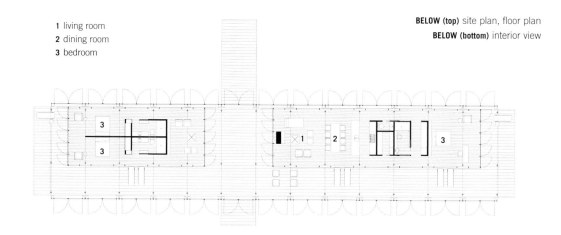

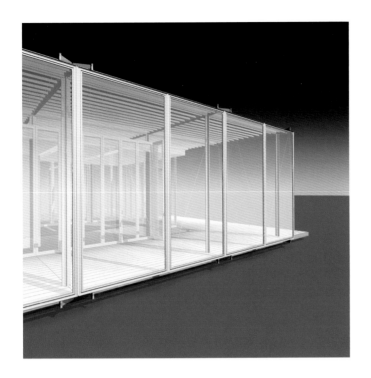
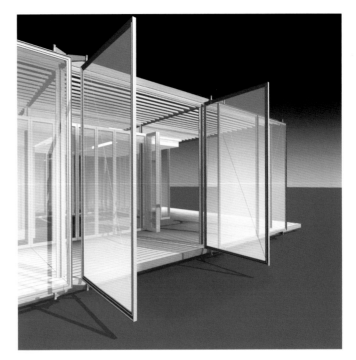

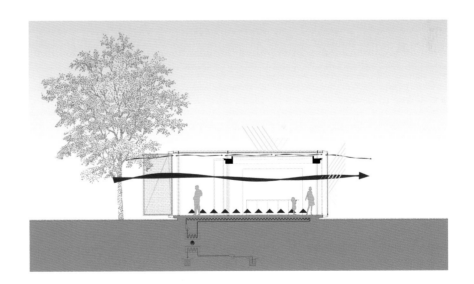

ABOVE screens, closed and open
RIGHT airflow diagram
OVERLEAF exterior view, screens closed

JESSE REISER & NANAKO UMEMOTO

RUR Architecture, PC   Sagaponac House 28   3,500 sq ft

Reiser + Umemoto's concept for Sagaponac House 28 is derived from their study of Mies van der Rohe's American houses, specifically the typology of the freestanding building. The sweeping lines of the house direct guests and residents along two connected arced walls: one that moves along the landscape and one that rises upward. Each wall culminates in the two main zones of the house. The arc of the formal entry stair rises gently up into the second story opening into a cantilevered living/dining room, a generous sunlit volume of space that soars over the landscape. The arc of the landscape wall directs residents and poolside guests through a glass door into a two-story foyer. This is the nexus of the house around which are arranged three bedrooms and a guest room, each in its own private volume. The master bedroom occupies a separate wing. It contains its own custom shower and bath area, which opens out onto a private garden from a sitting area. A generous walk-in closet within a sculptural wall separates the sitting area from the master bedroom beyond. These arcs thus define the principle volumes of the house, which communicate spatially through weaving.

While continuity at the volumetric level is achieved by this weaving, continuity among interior and exterior surfaces is achieved by introducing a striated geometry. This striation provides a system of repetition that is continuous, yet depending upon location, can acquire different materiality—from roof cladding on one extreme to turf on the other—the advantage of striation being that it provides a way of making smooth transitions from one material to another through meshing. Sagaponac House 28 thus becomes an extended elaboration of the way in which relations between inside and outside can be actualized through new architectural interpretations of a modernist precedent.

ABOVE aerial axonometric
OPPOSITE exterior view

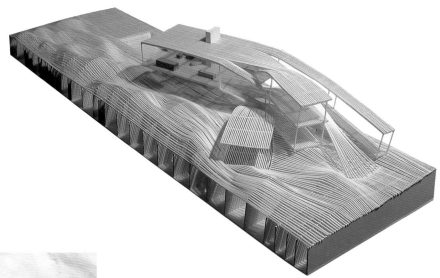

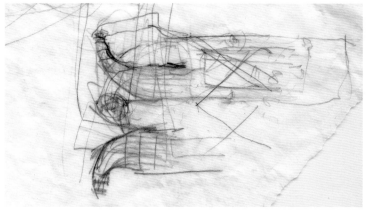

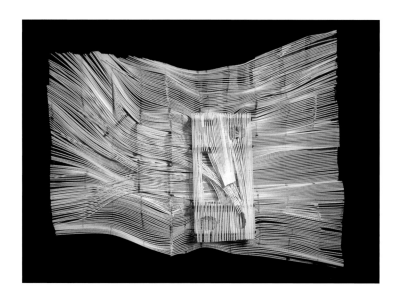

ABOVE contour model
LEFT concept model and concept sketch

RIGHT floor plans
BELOW model, poolside view

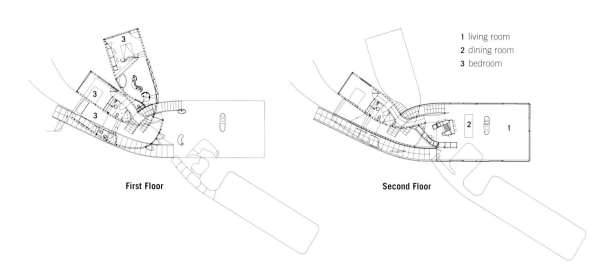

1 living room
2 dining room
3 bedroom

First Floor

Second Floor

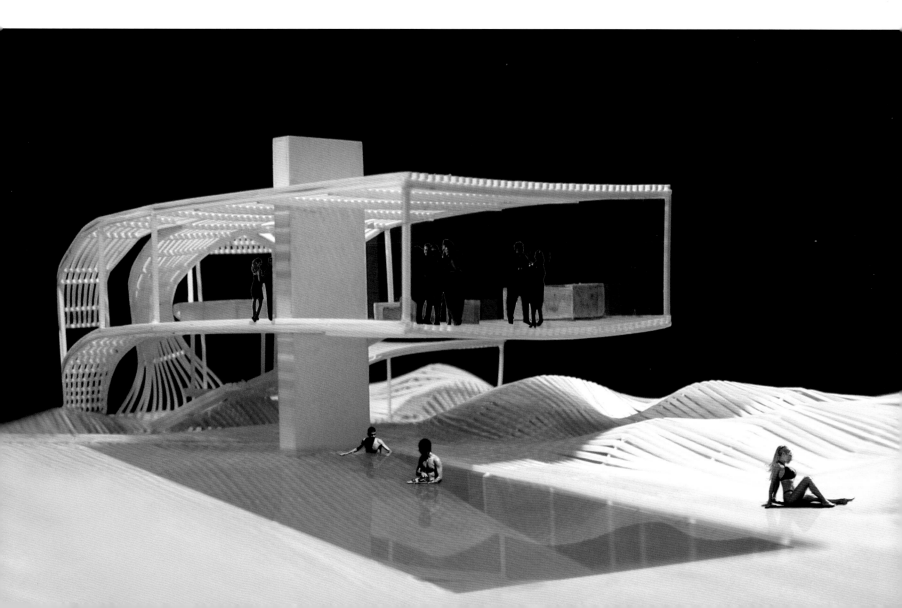

RICHARD ROGERS

Richard Rogers Partnership   Sagaponac House 30   3,000 sq ft

Richard Rogers' design for Sagaponac House 30 employs two main screen elements that cross each other at right angles to divide the site into four distinctive external spaces: a semiprivate entrance courtyard for receiving guests; a secluded service space for vehicles and utilities; a small, quiet garden for the occupants; and a large private space for relaxation, activities, and entertainment. The timber and stone screens vary in height, width, and opacity.

Inside the house, the screens define the geometry of the main spaces, not only acting as the main structural elements, supporting the roof, but also as internal spines along which key services are located. The heart of the house, the fireplace is symbolically located at the junction of these two walls. A small sitting area around the fireplace forms the pivot of the main living space. This living space is flexible, with minimum structural elements and can be opened fully to the private outdoor space. In summer, the living space can be further extended by opening the end wall to the swimming pool. When not in use, the pool provides a tranquil reflection of the house. The bedrooms are separated from the living room by the main service wall and all the bedrooms have views of the smaller, quiet garden.

Floating on top of the internal spaces is an insulated timber roof with overhangs made up of adjustable louvers that provide shading in summer and allow sunlight into the rooms in winter. A series of solar panels in the center of the roof provides most of the hot water requirement. Spaces between the top of the rooms and the underside of the roof allow for cross ventilation during hot seasons. With the glazed external walls opened, the swimming pool provides evaporative cooling to the living spaces. The house is raised above ground with an undercroft storage area that acts as a plenum with louvers which can be opened to cool the house in summer, and closed to provide insulation in winter. Warm air from the fireplace can also be directed to the plenum providing additional heating to other rooms in the house. Depending on the requirements of the future occupants, the swimming pool can also act as a heat sink to regulate the temperature inside the house.

LEFT sketch
OPPOSITE model, aerial view

176

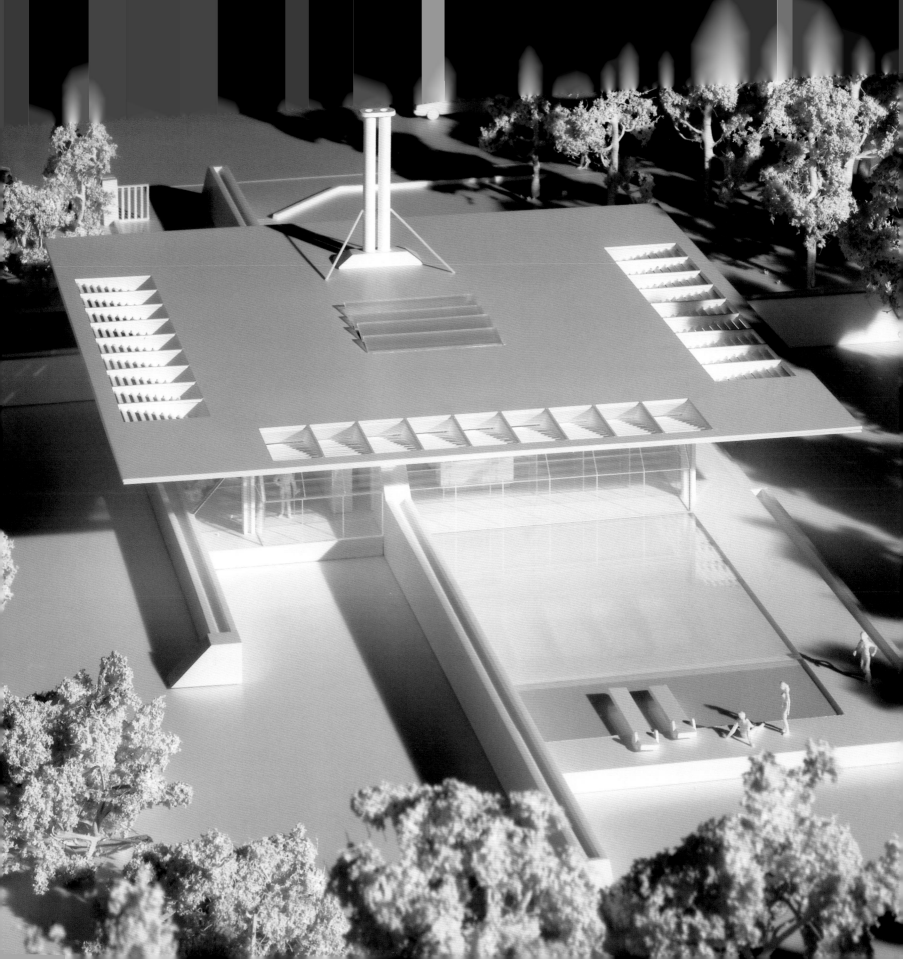

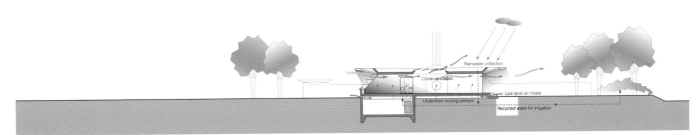

Summer Scenario

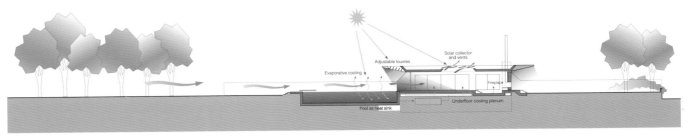

Summer Scenario

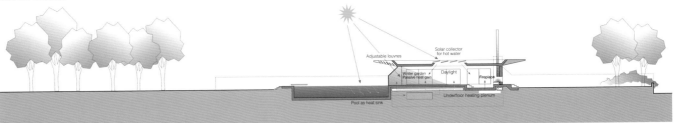

Winter Scenario

ABOVE view from southeast
RIGHT sketch
BELOW perspective from north

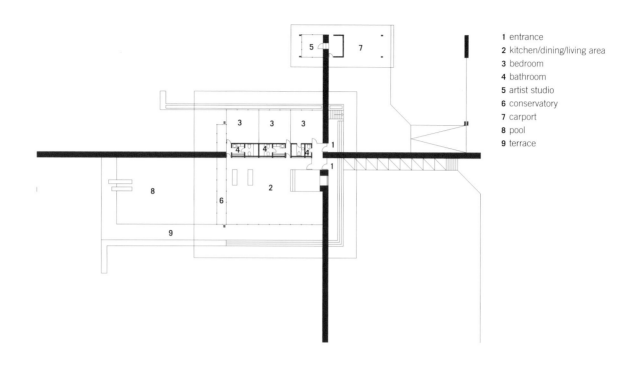

1 entrance
2 kitchen/dining/living area
3 bedroom
4 bathroom
5 artist studio
6 conservatory
7 carport
8 pool
9 terrace

ABOVE floor plan
BELOW perspective from southwest

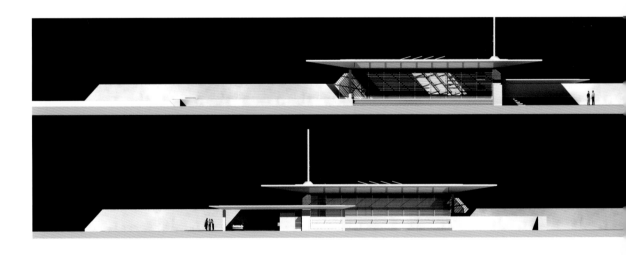

ABOVE view from northwest, entrance and carport
RIGHT east and west facades

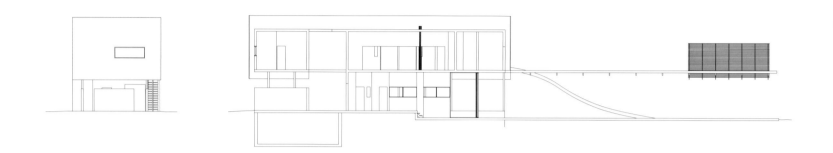

Michael Rotondi & Clark Philipp Stevens

RoTo Architects, Inc.   Sagaponac House 31   3,200 sq ft

Michael Rotondi and Clark Stevens's Sagaponac House 31 consists of a glass box, shaded and protected from the elements by an outer structure composed of laths. Large openings in the outer box permit access and views, while side gaps in between the wood boards filter sunlight to the interior during the day and appear as vertical strips of light at night. Organized on a four-foot module with primary structural spacing at eight and twelve feet, the house's walls and other elements are thin and as transparent or translucent as possible.

The house can be used year-round as a primary residence flexible enough to accommodate two to ten people. For public gatherings, the east end of the ground floor opens to the pool area and forest. The pool is a stone "quarry" with a shallow, sloping ground plane along its entire north side. When empty it will appear to be a natural part of the site. The bedroom suite above the carport, spatially separated from the main building, is connected by a breezeway to the second floor, accommodating a large sleeping area that can be subdivided as needed, and a lounge with a semi-public soaking tub and a slide into the pool. This upper lounge can function as a big "screened porch" when its windows on three sides are opened.

ABOVE west elevation, longitudinal section
OPPOSITE exterior perspectives

ABOVE poolside/living room perspective
BELOW floor plans

First Floor

Second Floor

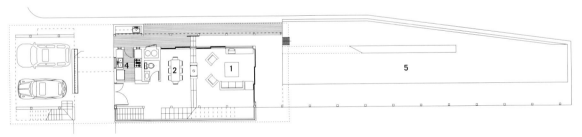

1 living room
2 dining room
3 bedroom
4 kitchen
5 pool

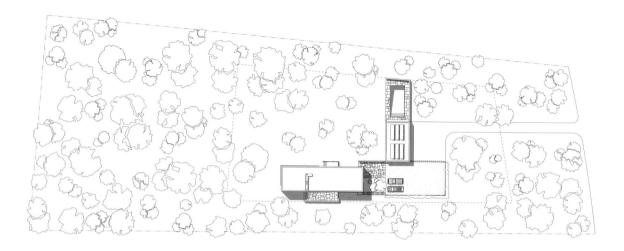

DANIEL ROWEN

Daniel Rowen Architects   Sagaponac House 32   4,000 sq ft

Sagaponac House 32 consists of two simple buildings: a residence and a studio. The relationship between them is a reinterpretation of a farmhouse and a barn, two common building types of the region. In this project, the barn has become a studio, designed to accommodate a wide range of creative uses. This modern barn is a place for activities that thrive beyond the boundaries of the residence. Like the farmhouse and barn, the residence and studio's separation is the key to both their coexistence and their identities.

The residence is a 3,000-square-foot, two-story building with a full basement. The ground floor includes a guest room, family room, and kitchen, with a gallery leading to a double-story living room. This space has a large corner window opening out toward the landscape. The second floor consists of a library, two bedrooms, and a master suite, which are accessed by a balcony corridor overlooking the gallery. The bedroom windows have adjustable wood louvers that provide privacy and modulate light.

The studio is a 1,000-square-foot space with north-facing skylights and eight pairs of large doors, four opening to a car court on one side and four opening to the landscape on the other side. Its open plan allows for the pursuit of a passion or a hobby that needs significant space and wants independence from the residence. It can be a garage, an art studio, a stable, a music room, a workshop, a greenhouse, or anything else that can fit within its walls. The studio's glass facade opens to a private terrace that can accommodate a garden or a pool.

The site is entered by a driveway that leads first to a car court that provides vehicular access to the studio, and then to an entry court that is shared by both buildings. In this way the studio also serves as a gate house to the property, shielding views of the residence and the grounds beyond. The residence is located along the side of the site so that the two buildings form an L shape, leaving the remainder of the property as a wooded landscape.

The materials of the project consist of two primary elements: a wood skin and a stone base. The residence is sheathed by a skin of cedar siding and mahogany window louvers. This envelope interlocks with a stone base whose topography becomes an interior landscape. The studio is a more static volume whose cedar siding and mahogany window details wrap a wood frame that rests on a flat stone floor. The consistency of this shared material palette allows the two buildings to differ in language, scale, and gesture, without losing their integrity as a unified whole.

ABOVE exterior perspective
OPPOSITE site plan

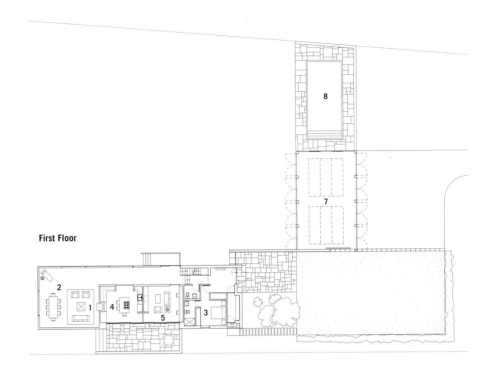

First Floor

Second Floor

1 living room
2 dining room
3 bedroom
4 kitchen
5 family
6 library
7 studio
8 pool

ABOVE model, aerial perspective
RIGHT floor plans
OPPOSITE exterior perspective

LINDY ROY

ROY Sagaponac House 33 3,700 sq ft

Eight S-shaped frames define the volume of the glass-and wood-clad Sagaponac House 33. The steel S-frames are organized in two groups placed perpendicular to one another, creating interlocking single- and double-height volumes. The S-shaped section allows the interior of the house to flow out to the garden while creating more enclosed, private spaces on the upper level. The concrete floor slabs of the dining and living rooms on the first floor continue outside. On the second floor, the curving profiles are clad in wood, creating modifiable louvered facades for the bedrooms and adjoining terraces.

A blue mosaic-tiled swimming pool penetrates the interior of the first floor, which houses a wet bar adjacent to the indoor pool and bathrooms. A sheet of water cascades from the study on the next level down into the pool. This "waterwall" screens off the more intimate space at the stair landing on the upper level where the three bedrooms, two with covered terraces, are located. The south-facing garden facade is all glass. Large sliding doors open the double-height dining area out to the poolside terrace, while large glass pivot doors extend the living room out to the garden on the east. A glass garage-type sliding door drops down to seal off the outside pool from the interior.

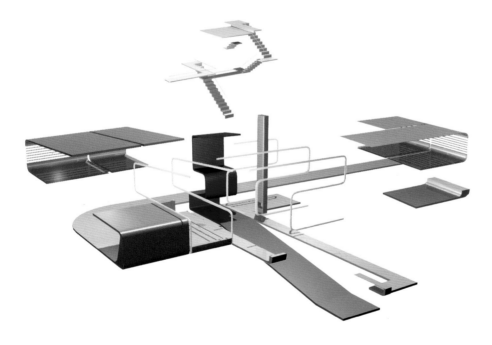

LEFT exploded perspective
OPPOSITE poolside elevation, night view

1 living room
2 dining room
3 bedroom
4 kitchen
5 terrace
6 indoor pool
7 pool

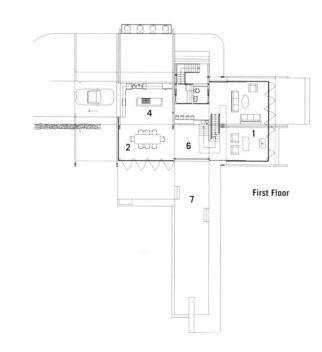

First Floor

Second Floor

ABOVE (top) exterior perspective
BELOW (bottom) floor plans

RIGHT conceptual ground
floor perspective
BELOW (left) site plan
BELOW (right) longitudinal section
OPPOSITE waterfall

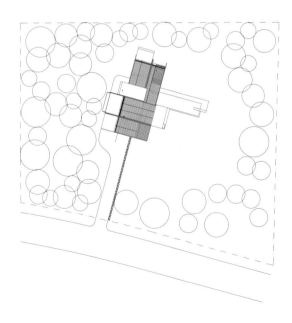

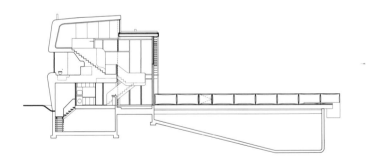

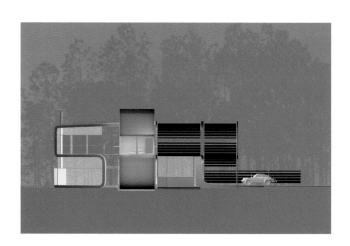

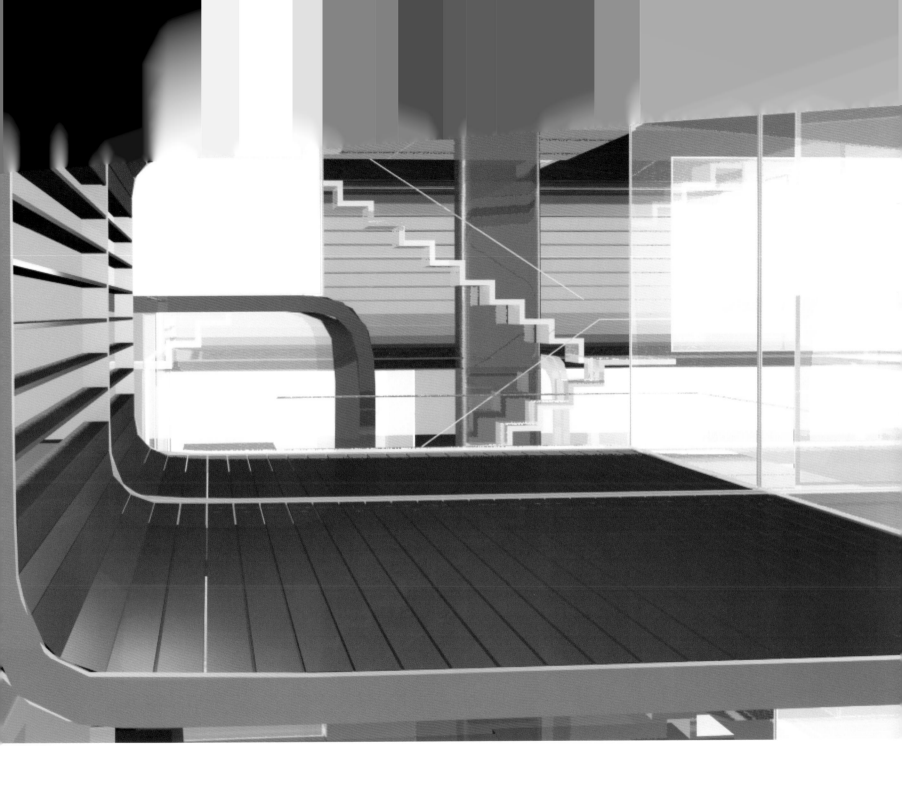

ANNABELLE SELLDORF

Selldorf Architects   Sagaponac House 34   3,300 sq ft

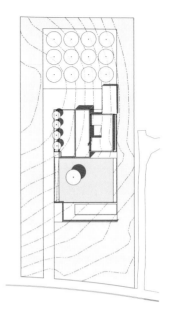

Selldorf Architects' design for the Sagaponac House 34 transforms a thickly over-grown plot, possessing a gentle slope but no impressive views, into a distinct layered environment, effectively changing it into a "micro landscape" within the existing growth of wild grasses and trees.

The program intertwines exterior and interior spaces and volumes. The house becomes an intrinsic element in the site, surrounded by a series of exterior rooms: a formal lawn with a raised terrace and pool to the south; a sunken flower garden to the west; and an apple orchard across the front yard to the north. It is anchored to a plinth of concrete, which extends to low retaining walls framing these spaces.

The square footprint of the house embodies the overall site strategy by defining exterior spaces within and adjacent to the building. The single-story wing is organized around a courtyard glazed on three sides to visually connect the public spaces: foyer, kitchen, living, and dining room. The bedrooms and study are located in a two-story wing that opens onto the sunken flower garden.

Consisting of simple timber frame and flat roof construction, the exterior is sheathed with clear cedar siding applied to achieve a taut appearance. Openings in the walls are a combination of large glass sliding doors and inward-opening French doors and casement windows. Steel frames are used for their minimal and elegant details.

The arrangement of exterior spaces is a reflection of the carefully proportioned plan both in terms of interior volumes and circulation, so that house and garden are perceived as a unified whole.

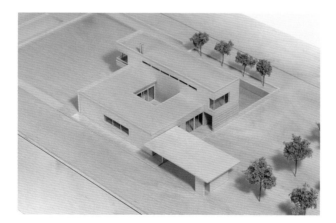

ABOVE site plan
LEFT aerial perspective
OPPOSITE exterior perspective

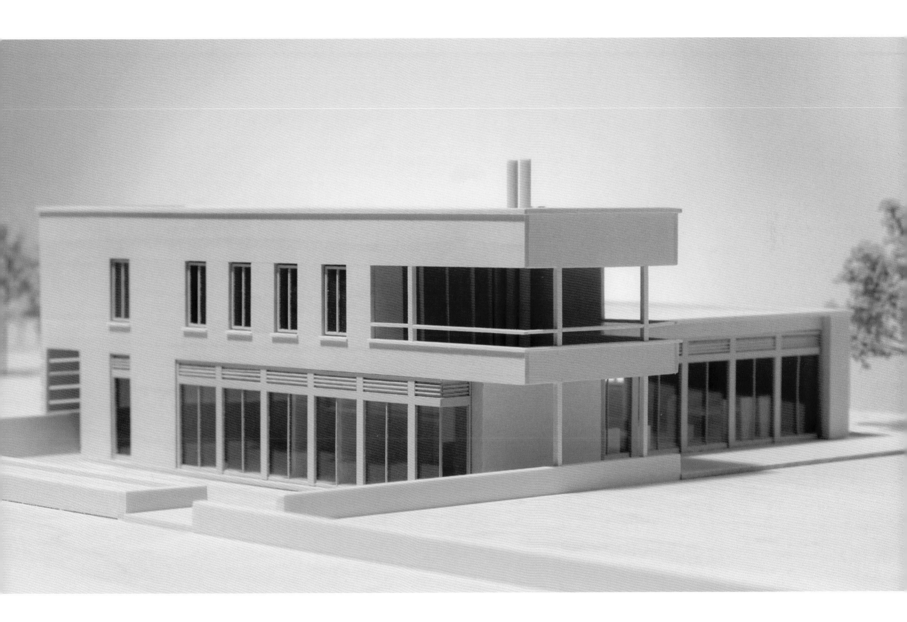

First Floor

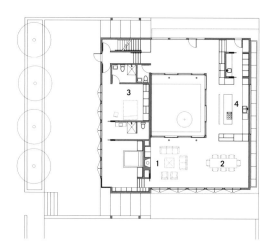

Second Floor

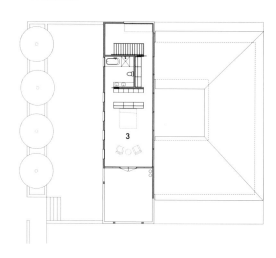

1 living room
2 dining room
3 bedroom
4 kitchen

ABOVE exterior perspective
LEFT floor plans

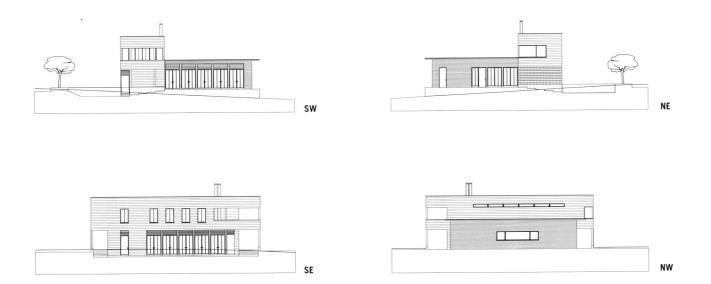

SW

NE

SE

NW

HENRY SMITH-MILLER & LAURIE HAWKINSON

Smith-Miller + Hawkinson Architects   Sagaponac House 35   3,300 sq ft

Smith-Miller + Hawkinson's design for Sagaponac House 35 rethinks the typical Long Island suburban house with a plan that appropriates and internalizes the majority of the site. No longer modeled on the American "House of the Prairie," front and rear yards are joined to create a court that slips under the house. The fusion of back to front morphs the public and private landscapes of the single-family house, creating a new model for the "subdivision." The garage space becomes (formal) entry, internalizing and showcasing the automobile, the Weber Grille, and the usual leisure equipment, all in the context of an extended and private court.

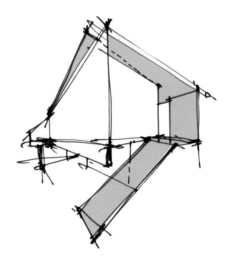

ABOVE collage and massing study
LEFT conceptual sketch
OPPOSITE aerial perspective

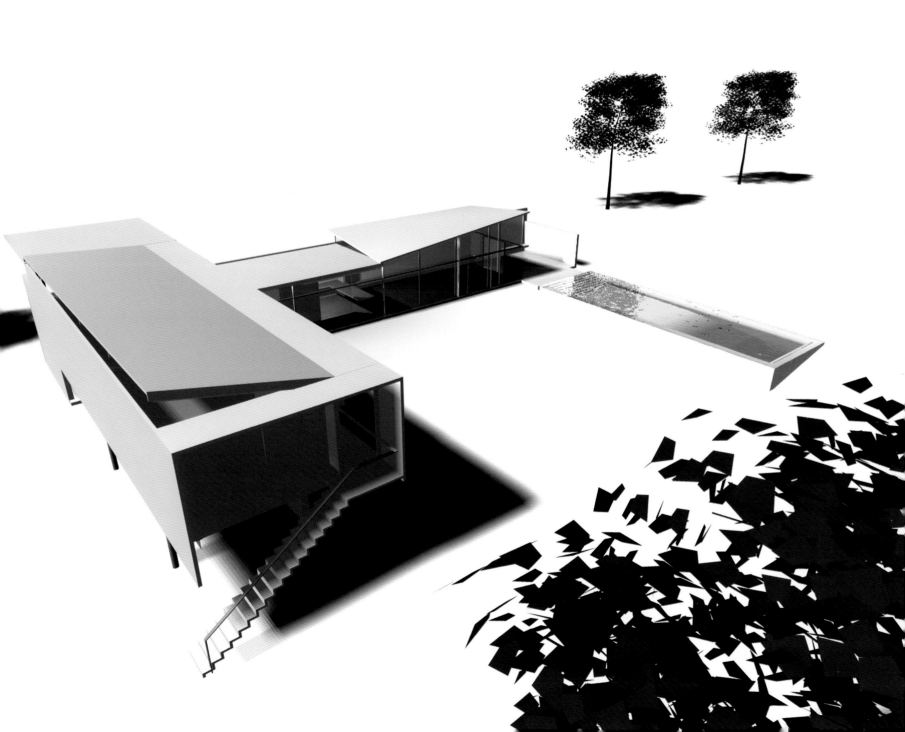

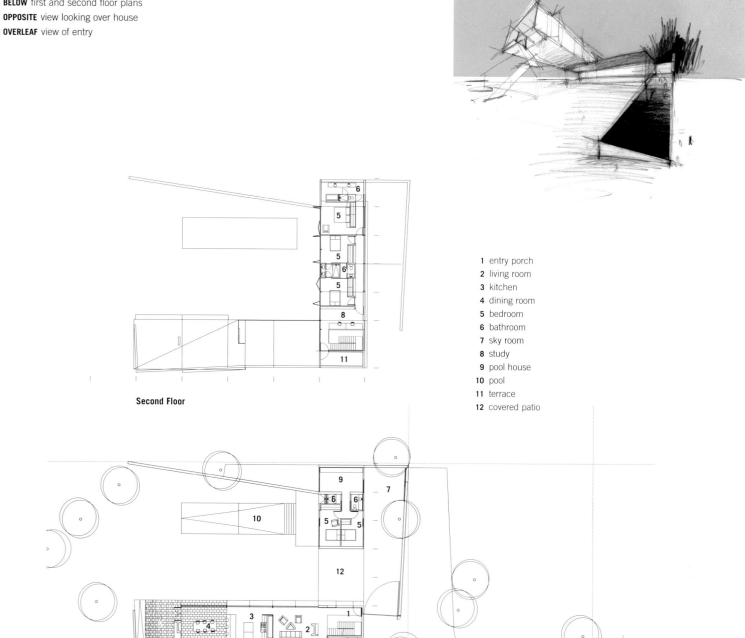

RIGHT sketch looking southwest
BELOW first and second floor plans
OPPOSITE view looking over house
OVERLEAF view of entry

Second Floor

1 entry porch
2 living room
3 kitchen
4 dining room
5 bedroom
6 bathroom
7 sky room
8 study
9 pool house
10 pool
11 terrace
12 covered patio

First Floor

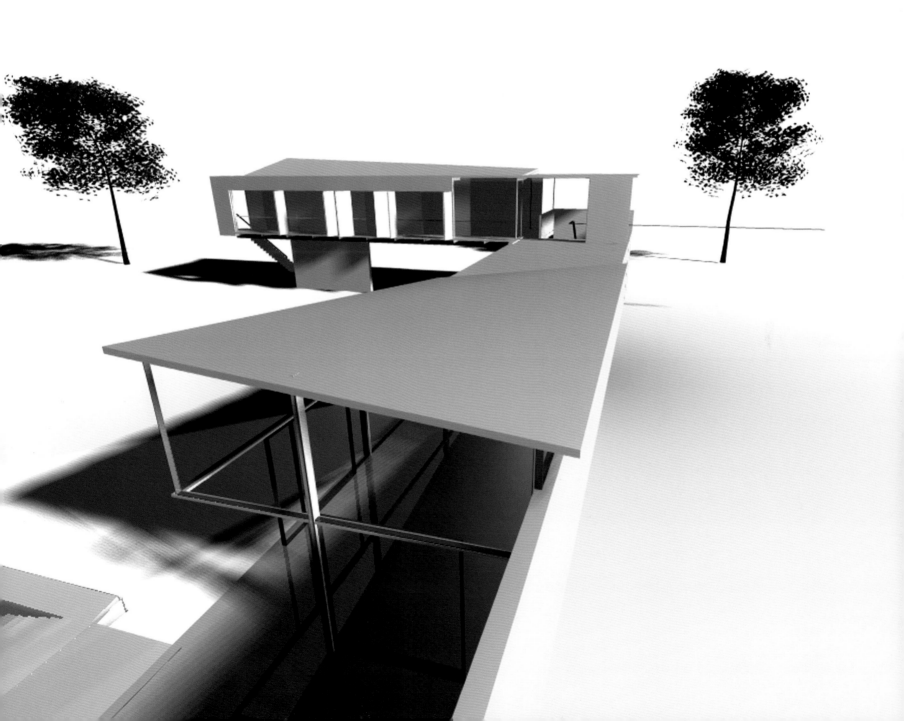

ABOVE model, aerial perspective
RIGHT sketch, aerial perspective

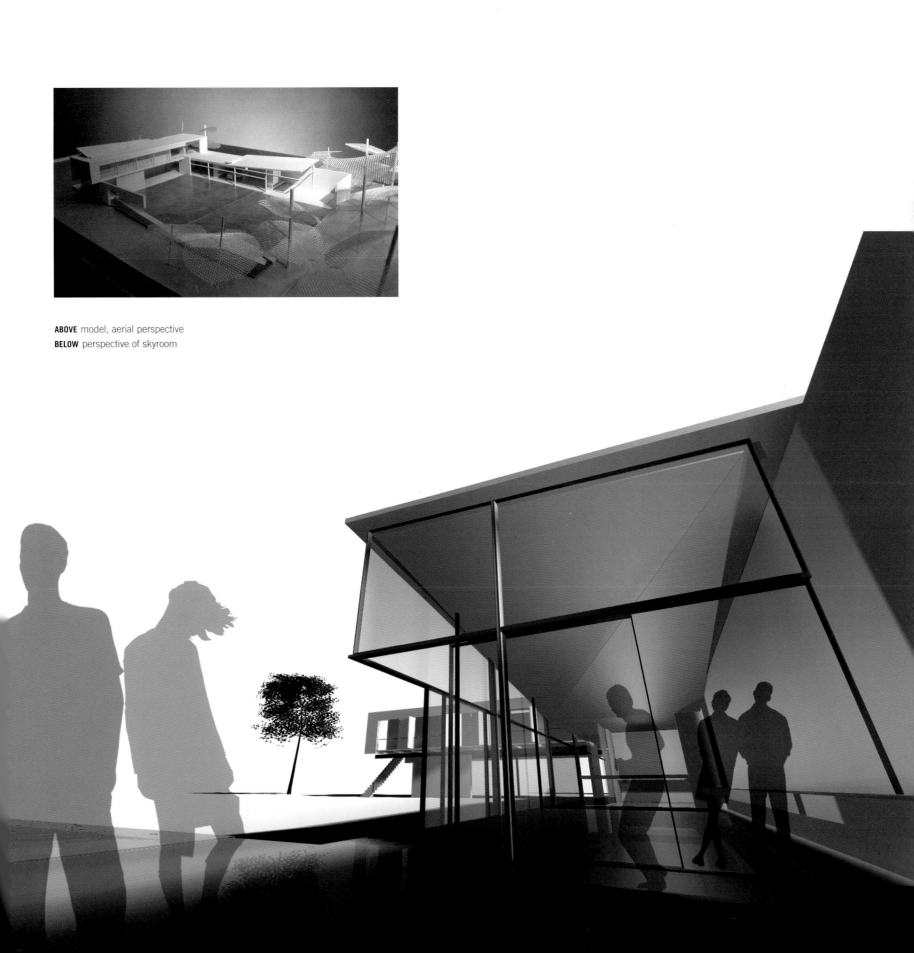

ABOVE model, aerial perspective
BELOW perspective of skyroom

CALVIN TSAO & ZACK MCKOWN

Tsao & McKown Architects, PC   Sagaponac House 36   4,500 sq ft

The evenly wooded and nearly flat site of Sagaponac House 36 highlighted two core issues for Tsao and McKown: the relative volume/bulk of the house in proportion to its bit of earth, and privacy versus views in and out of the site. It was also important to firmly root the house to the site.

Programmatic issues proved helpful in generating Tsao and McKown's overall approach. The house would most likely have to serve widely varying needs: sometimes as a retreat for two (or one) and at other times as host to many guests, spanning generations and including various subsets of families and friends.

Somewhat paradoxically, perhaps, the one house wants to become two. The domain of the primary inhabitants (most likely a couple) rises above the ground as a modest wood and glass cube, an object building that reinterprets the basic four walls and roof of the iconic house.

On the first level are the formal entry, double-height living and dining spaces, and kitchen. Stacked above, in a play of single and double-height volumes, are a guest bedroom (or study) and a master suite. At the treetop level is a private roof terrace with an integral movable screen to shield excess sun and breezes. Below, to create the distinct second zone and to anchor the house to the site, the architects carve into the earth to create what is effectively an additional (but more private) ground level, where a non-object house comprised of a series of spaces organized around outdoor rooms accommodates informal entry, living, dining, kitchen, lounge, and additional guest bedrooms. Automobile entry and storage is also handled at this lower level (but on the north side), conveniently and completely removing that equipment from view. The house is unexpectedly expansive, yet protected, as the operable glass walls of these large spaces open onto sunny terraces, pool, and sloping lawns.

Second Floor

Mezzanine

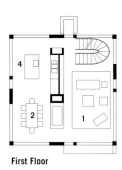

First Floor

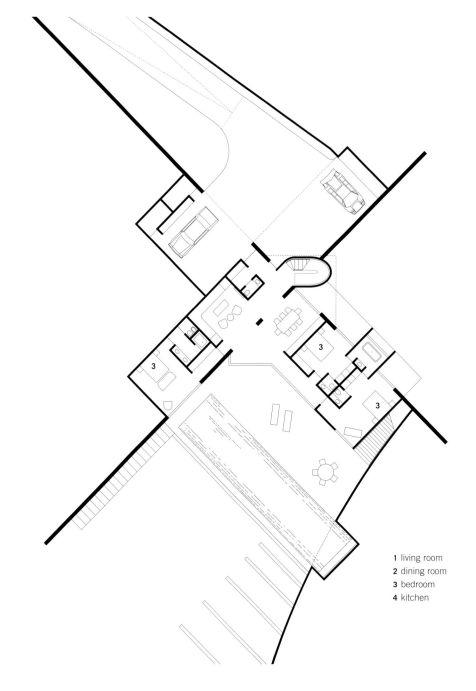

1 living room
2 dining room
3 bedroom
4 kitchen

JEAN-MICHEL WILMOTTE

Wilmotte & Associes   Sagaponac House 37   3,800 sq ft

Sagaponac House 37 is composed of two massive volumes flanking a third central volume, distributing the villa. The progression from the street to the house crosses landscaped sequences. Beyond the entrance, two staircases and a footbridge access the rest of the house.

The entrance volume is defined by two walls: the first opaque, ensuring the privacy of the inhabitants; the second transparent, overlooking the pool and landscape. The view to the garden is framed from the two residential wings. The massive white walls are cut into by slits and full windows. These openings let light flow in and create a play of solids and voids. The white of the materials reinforces the effect of the simple volumes varied by light and sun.

ABOVE aerial perspective
OPPOSITE entrance view

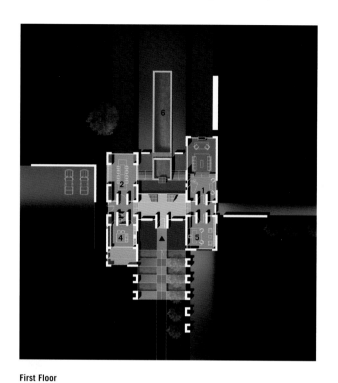

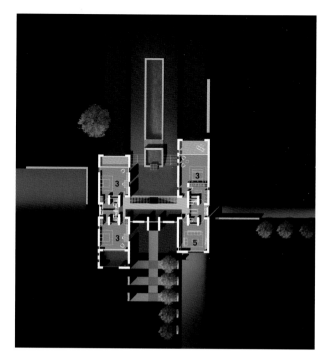

1 living room
2 dining room
3 bedroom
4 kitchen
5 office
6 pool

First Floor

Second Floor

ABOVE floor plans
LEFT exterior elevation
OPPOSITE view from garden

ARCHITECTS

Field Operations
274 Water Street
New York, NY 10038

232 North 2nd Street
Philadelphia, PA 19106
www.fieldoperations.net

Stan Allen, *Principal;* Matt Schnepf, *Project Architect*

Marwan Al-Sayed Architects
4411 North 40th Street, #56
Phoenix, AZ 85081
www.masastudio.com

Marwan Al-Sayed, *Principal & Project Designer;* Mies Grybaitis, *Partner/Artist;* Amit Upadhye, *Schematic Design;* Joby Dutton, *Construction Documents/Renderings/Model;* Thomas Hartman, *Renderings;* Marianna Athanasiadou, *Renderings*

Anthony Ames Architect
19 East 72nd Street
New York, NY 10021

PO Box 54144,
Atlanta, GA 30308

Anthony Ames, *Principal;* Clark Tefft, *Design Assistant;* Alan Brown, *Computer*

Shigeru Ban Architects + Dean Maltz Architect
Ban Building 5-2-4 Matsubara
Setagaya-Ku, Tokyo
Japan 15400

330 West 38th Street, Suite 811
New York, NY 10018
www.dnp.co.jp/millennium/SB/
Van_e.html and www.dma-ny.com

Shigeru Ban, *Principal;* Dean Maltz, *Principal;* Andrew Lefkowitz, *Project Architect;* Tamaki Terai, *Project Architect;* Paul Gentry, *Model Photos*

Deborah Berke & Partners Architects LLP

211 West 19th Street, 2nd Floor
New York, NY 10011
www.dberke.com

Deborah Berke, *Principal;* Steven Brockman,
Project Architect; Matt Kelley, *Design Team;*
Noah Biklen, *Design Team;* Stephane Le
Blanc, *Design Team*

Francois de Menil Architect, PC

1140 Broadway Suite 704
New York, NY 10001
www.fdmarch.com

Francois De Menil, *Project Designer &
Principal;* David Marin, *Design Team;* Susan
de Menil, *Design Team;* Richard Snyder,
Design Team

Antonio Citterio and Partners

Via Cerva 4
Milano, Italy 20122
www.antoniocitterioandpartners.it

Antonio Citterio, *Principal;* Patricia Viel,
Partner

Pei Cobb Freed & Partners Architects LLP

88 Pine Street
New York, NY 10005
www.pcf-p.com

James Ingo Freed, *Principal;* Elizabeth
Polenz, *Associate;* Kyle Humphries,
Renderings; John Dosier, *Renderings*

Pei Cobb Freed & Partners Architects LLP

88 Pine Street
New York, NY 10005
www.pcf-p.com

Henry Cobb, *Principal;* David Bae, *Associate;*
Anca Vasiliu, *Project Intern*

Gluckman Mayner Architects

250 Hudson Street, 10th Floor
New York, NY 10013
www.gluckmanmayner.com

Richard Gluckman, *Principal;* Greg Yang,
Project Architect; Dean Young, *Architect*

11

Michael Graves & Associates

341 Nassau Street
Princeton, NJ 08504

560 Broadway, Suite 401
New York, NY 10012
www.michaelgraves.com

Michael Graves, *Principal;* John Diebboll,
Principal-in-charge; Bob Miller, *Project
Manager;* Ester Kardos, *Designer*

14

Hariri & Hariri - Architecture

18 East 12th Street, Ground Floor
New York, NY 10003
www.haririandhariri.com

Gisue Hariri, *Pricipal;* Mojgan Hariri,
Principal; Thierry Pfister, *Project Architect;*
Markus Randler, *Project Architect*

12

Zaha Hadid Architects

Studio 9
10 Bowling Green Lane
London EC1R OBQ
www.zaha-hadid.com

Zaha Hadid, *Principal & Project Designer;*
Markus Dochantschi, *Project Manager;*
Stephane Hos, *Senior Architect;* Patrick
Schumacher, *Director;* Barbara
Pfenningstorff, *Architect;* Tiago Correia,
Architect; Ana Cajiao, *Architect;* Ken
Bostock, *Architect*

15

Steven Harris Architects

50 Warren Street
New York, NY 10007
www.stevenharrisarchitects.com

Steven Harris, *Principal;* Drew Lang, *Project
Architect;* Will Tim, *Project Assistant;* David
Kelly, *Project Assistant;* Mig Perkins,
Renderer; Victoria Partridge, *Renderer*

13

Hanrahan + Meyers Architects

22 West 21st Street, 12th Floor
New York, NY 10010
www.hanrahanmeyers.com

Thomas Hanrahan, *Project Designer &
Principal;* Victoria Meyers, *Project Designer
& Principal;* Lawrence Zeroth, *Team Member*

16

Hodgetts + Fung

5837 Adams Boulevard
Culver City, CA 90232
www.hplusf.com

Craig Hodgetts, *Principal;* Hsin-ming Fung,
Principal; Neil Silberstein, *Designer;* Thierry
Garzotto, *Design Team*

Steven Holl Architects

450 West 31st Street, 11th Floor
New York, NY 10001
www.stevenholl.com

Steven Holl, *Principal & Project Designer;*
Annette Goderbauer, *Project Architect;* The
Orchard Group, *Model*

Robert Kahn Architect

611 Broadway, Suite 201
New York, NY 10012

Robert Kahn, *Principal-in-charge;* Tommy Lee
White, *Project Architect;* Sergio Bregante,
Project Team

Carlos Jimenez Studio

1116 Willard Street
Houston, TX 77006

Carlos Jimenez, *Principal;* Cris Ruebush,
Design Team

Kanner Architects

10924 Le Conte Avenue
Los Angeles, CA 90024
www.kannerarch.com

Stephen H. Kanner, *Design Principal/ Project
Designer;* David Ellien, *Project Designer,
Renderings/Presentation Drawings;* Alex
Dunn, *Project Architect*

Philip Johnson/Alan Ritchie Architects

375 Park Avenue
New York, NY 10152
www.pjar.com

Philip Johnson, *Principal;* Alan Ritchie,
Principal-in-charge; Ken Lin, *Associate;*
Hiroshi Nakamura, *Project Manager;* Peter
Liesandt, *Senior Architect;* Paul Gentry,
Model Photos

Keenen/Riley (K/R)

526 West 26th Street
New York, NY 10001
www.krnyc.com

John Keenen, *Principal;* Terence Riley,
Principal; Nathan McRae; Raul Smith;
Katerina Chatzikonstantinou

Richard Meier & Partners

475 Tenth Avenue
New York, NY 10018
www.richardmeier.com

Richard Meier, *FAIA*; Lisetta Koe, *Director of Communications*

MVRDV

Schiehaven 15
3024 EC Rotterdam NL
Postbus 63136
www.mvrdv.nl

Winy Maas, *Principal*; Jacob van Rijs, *Principal*; Nathalie de Vries, *Principal*
Marc Joubert; Jeroen Zuidgeest
Joanna Gasparski; Nicolas Sowers; Bart Spee

Samuel Mockbee Architect

360 E. North Street
Kanton, MS 39046

Samuel Mockbee, *Project Designer & Principal*; G. Williamson Archer, *Project Architect*; Farrol D. Hollomon, *Project Architect*; David Ford, *Intern Architect*; Paul Gentry, *Model photos*

Thomas Phifer and Partners

180 Varick Street
New York, NY 10014
www.tphifer.com

Thomas Phifer, *Prinicipal*; Greg Reaves, *Project Architect*; Christoph Timm, *Project Designer*; dBox, *Renderings*

Eric Owen Moss Architects

8557 Higuera Street
Culver City, CA 90232
www.ericowenmoss.com

Eric Owen Moss, *Principal*; Don Dimster, *Project Architect*; Eric McNevin, *Project Architect*; Andy Liu; John Bencher; Mark Salin; Emil Mertzel; Dolan Daggett; Eugene Slobodyanyuk; Susanne Kortz; Jin-Bum Kim; Grit Leipert

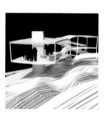

RUR Architecture

118 East 59th Street, Suite 402
New York, NY 10022
www.reiser-umemoto.com

Jesse Reiser, *Principal*; Nanako Umemoto, *Principal*; Rhett Russo, *Principal Designer*; Eva Perez Derega, *Principal Designer*; Jason Scroggin, *Team Member*; Matthias Blass, *Team Member*

Cooper Robertson & Partners
311 West 43rd Street
New York, NY 10036
www.cooperrobertson.com

Jaquelin T. Robertson, *Principal*

Daniel Rowen Architects
448 West 37th Street, 12B
New York, NY 10018
www.computersandimaging.com/
drindex.html

Daniel Rowen, *Principal-in-charge;*
Alessandro Ayuso; Jeremy Barbour; Jose
Coriano; Michael Nolan; John Ottinger

Richard Rogers Partnership
Thames Wharf
Rainville Road
London W6 9HA
www.rrp.co.uk

Richard Rogers, *Design Team;* Laurie Abbott,
Design Team; Dennis Ho, *Design Team;* Mimi
Hawley, *Design Team;* Mike Fairbrass, *Model;*
Tim Mason, *Model;* Melon Studio, *3D Images*

ROY
833 Washington Street, Suite 4
New York, NY 10014
www.roydesign.com

Lindy Roy, *Principal;* Mark Kroeckel,
Openshop/Studio, *Project Architect;* Jason
Lee, *Project Architect;* Barbara Ludescher,
Project Team; Gernot Riether, *Project Team;*
Monica Tiulescu, *Project Team;* Louise Vrou,
Project Team

RoTo
600 Moulton Avenue, Suite 405
Los Angeles, CA 90031
www.rotoark.com

Michael Rotondi, *Principal;* Clark Stevens,
Principal; Ha Seung Choi, *Project Architect*

Selldorf Architects
62 White Street
New York, NY 10013
www.selldorf.com

Annabelle Selldorf, *Principal;* Anne Nixon,
Project Manager; Matt Schneph, *Project
Architect*

35

Smith-Miller + Hawkinson Architects

305 Canal Street
New York, NY 10013
www.smharch.com

Henry Smith-Miller, *Principal;* Laurie Hawkinson, *Principal;* Luben Dimcheff, *Project Architect*

36

Tsao & McKown Architects, PC

20 Vandam Street, 10th Floor
New York, NY 10013
www.tsao-mckown.com

Calvin Tsao, *Principal;* Zach McKown, *Principal;* Adam Rolston, *Senior Associate;* Kyo Chin, *Architect*

37

Wilmotte & Associes

68 Rue du Faubourg Saint-Antoine
75012 Paris, France
www.did.net/data/scripts/company/
index.idc?Company_no=2084

Jean Michel Wilmotte, *Principal*

Structural Engineers

Robert Silman Associates
Consulting Engineers
88 University Place
New York, NY 10003-4542

The Brown Companies

461 Park Avenue South
New York, NY 10016
www.housesatsagaponac.com

Coco Brown, *Developer*
Paula Willson, *Project Director*
Sunitha Kondur Ramachandran,
Senior Project Manager
Peggy Hsu, *Project Manager*
Jayda Uras, *Project Designer*
Damien Yoo, *Graphic Designer*
Caryn Koster, *Asst. Project Manager*
Danielle Adornato, *Project Intern*
Dana Dart-Mclean, *Project Intern*
Antonia Thompson, *Project Intern*
Timothy B. Mcauley, *Project Intern*